THE AMAZING KRESKIN'S FUTURE WITH THE STARS

by Kreskin
with Bret Saxon

THE AMAZING KRESKIN'S FUTURE WITH THE STARS
copyright © 2001
by Kreskin
All rights reserved
Printed in the United States of America

Many thanks to Howard Rapp, who made this all possible.

Editorial Assistance by Diane D. Pugliese

Cover by Gerry Mulhall

ISBN 0-916638-53-7

Distributed to the trade by
Meyerbooks
P.O. Box 427
Glenwood, IL 60425

TABLE OF CONTENTS

HEALTH & SCIENCE

Benjamin Luntz – Physicist
Shifu Robert Redfeather – Master of Tie
Grand Master Clifford C. Crandall, Jr.
Dr. Joyce Brothers
Buzz Aldrin – Astronaut
Dr. Lucy Jones – Earthquake Specialist
Dr. Edward Teller – Developed the Atomic Bomb
Debra W. Heffner – Human Sexuality
Raymond Porter – Natural Gas Expert
Gerard V. Sunnen, M.D. – Scientist of the Mind
Wulf H. Utian, M.D., Ph. D. – Menopause Research
Seymour Fish, D.D.S. – Dentistry
Alan M. MacRobert – Astronomer
Berthold E. Schwarz, M.D. – Para-Normal Expert
David Satcher, M.D., Ph.D. – Ass't. Secretary
   for Surgeon General
Alan Caruba – National Anxiety Center
Warren Eckstein – Pet Therapist
Dr. Paul Kurtz – Philosophy
Cote & Hall – National Fire Prevention Assoc.
Sally E. Smith – Fat Acceptance, Inc.

MISCELLANEOUS

Alan Greenspan – Chairman of the Federal Reserve Bank
Wolfgang Puck – Chef to the Stars
Arthur Friedman – Fashion
Casey Bush – Headwear Information Bureau
Larry Helton – Educator
Pat Robertson – Religious Leader
Phil Blazer – Publisher
Fairda Sharan – Spiritual Leader
Father Joseph Livolsi
Melvin Slavick – Sculptor
Ray Ferry – Publisher
Robert Collins – Publisher
Nick Meglin – Editor
David Meyer – Publisher
Frederik Pohl – Writer
Ruth Stafford Peale – Magazines
Barry A. Miller – Editor
John Romero – Gaming Expert
Dian Williams – Arson Research
Alexander M. Haig, Jr.

MORE ENTERTAINMENT

Regis Philbin
Arthur Godfrey
Steve Allen
Art Linkletter
Buddy Hackett
Phyllis Diller
David Brenner
Kathi Lee Gifford

First Impressions

I'll never forget the night I first met the Amazing Kreskin. My publisher was throwing a book release party for my latest authoring at a trendy New York club. The room was packed and there was little room to maneuver without bumping into someone. The crowd was having a good time and the event seemed very successful.

I was in the middle of speaking with a well-wisher, when my publisher rushed over to me and urgently said that someone had just arrived that I had to meet. As my publisher escorted me hurriedly towards the other side of the room he simply said, "The Amazing Kreskin is here!"

I had certainly heard of the Amazing Kreskin, and was aware of his truly incredible feats, but I had never had the pleasure of meeting him, nor had I seen his talent in action. As I approached him he was surrounded by a group that was clearly hanging on his every word. I noticed that he had his small social audience totally mesmerized by whatever story he was telling. My publisher barged into the circle and announced an introduction.

Kreskin stared into my eyes and I could feel him reaching into my mind. He extended his hand and I took it. To say his handshake is firm is to say the Titanic was a "big boat." If you aren't prepared, Kreskin will rip your arm off with his legendary handshake. We began talking.

An hour later, my publisher tried to interrupt, telling me that I should spend some time "working the room" as it was a party for my book and I had been focused completely on my conversations with Kreskin, ignoring the rest of the guests. Kreskin agreed, telling me we would talk later. I thanked him and slowly moved away.

As I began meeting others in the room, the conversations returned to the norm – "Your book is interesting," "How did you get the idea for your book," "What was it like when you were on *Dateline NBC*?" As the questions kept flowing, I found myself suddenly realizing how predictable all of these conversations were. I found myself thinking back to my conversation with Kreskin.

I spend my time meeting people - - interacting and communicating.

KRESKIN'S IMPRESSIONS

This book was to appear almost two years ago in the later months of 1999. It may have been providence and a quiet blessing that the book was delayed by the turbulence in the publishing industry. I consider it a tremendous benefit as it enabled me to add these reflections and point out what a pivotal point the book is in what is the true millennium which is 2001 AD

In the year 2000, yours truly took on a self-imposed challenge which neither the Nostredamus' nor the Jeanne Dixon's etc. have ever been nervy o r foolhardy enough to attempt. I appeared on the national radio and television show, The Howard Stern Show, with an envelope containing what was to be the result of the national presidential election. That envelope was delivered to Stern, on August 8, 2000, in the presence of Detective Ken Otto of the Bergenfield, N. J. Police Department, who knew the contents of that envelope. Indeed, quietly, yours truly had also sent copies to five prominent people in the U. S.

It was a 50/50 attempt however, and I was so certain that I enclosed in the envelope a check for $100,000. Should yours truly have failed, the check would have been cashed by Howard Stern and donated to his favorite charity. One can only imagine the mixed emotions I experienced: disappointment to exhilaration to modified horror, as a month later on election night I watched the results. First seeing Gore "win" and then Bush, at which point I decided to call a number of people and explain that I had succeeded in my targeted prediction. Needless to say not long after, I saw the certainty of who was to be president, in question. As it turned out, Bush won, which was as I had predicted. I also attempted to determine the amount of states Bush would carry. I projected 32 states, and in my statement, said I could be off by one or two. Bush carried 30 states, though with the counts and recounts…Stern also reminded the audience that I had made a prediction preceding this.

On January 1, 1999, on CNN, I made a statement, which was initially pooh-poohed by many political stalwarts; namely that Hillary Rodham Clinton would run for office in the United States Senate from the State of New York and would win. This prediction was reiterated by me hundreds of times in radio, TV and public appearances in the months that ensued before the election. By now of course, you all know the results. On January 1, 2000, on CNN, yours truly predicted that Bill Gates would step down from Microsoft, sometime in the next 14 or so days. 12 days later a bulletin flashed across CNN, that Bill Gates had stepped down. The bulletin ended: "Thank you Kreskin!"

Parenthetically, one more prediction was made on January 1, 2000 that before the end of the year 2000, a historic 1st in sports history would take place: a quarter of a billion-dollar contract would be signed. In December 2000, Alex Rodriguez signed a $252,000,000 contract with the Texas Rangers.

This book has for me taken on far more meaning. There are the trivial, superficial predictions, which can be smiled at or even ignored. Perhaps a few would fit in the gossip column. But, beyond this there is a strange meaningful intrigue about certain parties, who contributed since they first submitted to me their contribution. Since their writing, Kathie Lee is no longer with a job she had for many years on ABC-TV with Regis Philbin. John Gambling, radio legend, whose work on WOR was preceded by his father and grandfather through many, many years, is no longer at that broadcasting venue. And, as if it were the last expression in public utterance, Steve Allen, the legendary raconteur humorist and philosopher of television has given us his last reflections. I believe that this book, if you will savor certain areas, will have some truly meaningful and fascinating projections.

KRESKIN

KRESKIN INTRODUCTION

This book has been the fulfillment of a dream. I have spoken to so many people who agree that the concept for this book is truly unique, especially considering that we are approaching a new century. This is not simply a "celebrity book", a fluff piece on the latest movie and television stars. We can find every aspect of their lives and opinions fully examined by the tabloids, both in print and on television. I am not sure that you, nor I, would be quick to purchase a book full of such exploits which would probably be out of date before it even reached the newsstands and the book stores.

This is a book of celebrated individuals from every walk of life, whose activities have influenced, interested, and touched us from time to time. It is their reflections and speculations as to how their profession or area of expertise will change in the coming century that are explored in this volume. Is that not as realistic and credible a form of prophecy as one can imagine? No crystal balls were used in the creation of this book, no special taro cards were read - just thoughtful predictions by those at the top of their fields. Would you really want an astrologer to tell you the changes that will be taking place in the next few years in the field of medicine? I am not sure that I would want a numerologist to explain to me what my personal safety problems or that of my family will be in the years of 2000. Many of the people in this book will be unknown to you, but rest assured, from my own knowledge of their work, or from knowing them personally, they are indeed the experts and authorities in their own field.

There was a time early in my career when I discounted anything dealing with prophecy. I considered such theories occult hogwash. In those early days you could have described me as a typical square-headed, narrow-minded skeptic. Fifty years ago I would have spouted the typical trite sayings of the naysayers - "extraordinary claims require extraordinary proof" and the like. However, as I left the specialty of magic and conjuring and embraced more and more the mentalist aspects of my career, it became clear to me that people can look into the future. Indeed, many people have this ability, and it isn't as dark and mysterious as a cursory view might dictate.

I was foolish to deny the possibility that people have the ability to predict future occurrences. I can offer proof immediately - weathermen have been doing it for years! They have been projecting through their own area of expertise. What they foresee is not the "free future" but the "controlled future." Through sophisticated techniques they become aware of conditions that can lead to weather patterns that will appear in the upcoming hours, days, and weeks to come. The questions then become, "Why can't a sociologist do the same thing?" Or, "Why can't a physicist predict advances in his field?"

Obviously, the authoritative people who grace this book believe in some form of prophecy, otherwise they would be hypocrites. This book does not contain vague verses in which you can apply any interpretation, either today or a thousand years from now. The projections contained in this book are specific and in many cases, dramatic. I don't think you will easily be able to turn away from the prophecies from the experts contained in this book - I know I certainly couldn't.

My first entry for this book was actually written some thirty years ago - long before I ever envisioned writing a book on the predictions of the knowledgeable and wise in our culture. In 1968, 1 was performing at Chautauqua in New York State. Chautauqua boasts a semi-enclosed theater that hosts events for those interested in cultural discussions, scientific topics and philosophical areas of thought. The events were attended by both students and vacationers from all over the country. The evening I walked out on stage I noticed that in the front row, holding a large staff, was a legend -- Dr. Margaret Mead. Dr. Mead, who stands almost six feet tall, was an anthropologist extraordinaire -- a true woman of the world. Whatever the issue, it was not unusual to find Dr. Mead appearing on television or radio giving her take on the controversy. Her interests were vast.

I was very familiar with Dr. Mead, as she had gained attention for convincing an international scientific organization into accepting parapsychology as a worthy area of investigation. The scientific community was under intense pressure to reject Dr. Mead's assertions. However, by sheer force of personality she was able to persuade the officials to be more open to the unknown. She would be a formidable adversary against the organized skeptics that proliferate today. In her own way, she had a gift of leveling people with a simple glance or a single truism. As an example, I attended a conference she was holding for a few thousand students. I sat in the back and was absolutely spellbound. Towards the end of Dr. Mead's question and answer session, a student of the 60's culture raised his hand and asked, "Dr. Mead, what do you think of the new morality?" Dr. Mead stared directly into the eyes of the student and simply said, "Do you mean new morality, or no morality?" There was dead silence in the hall, and then thunderous applause. There isn't a skeptic of parapsychology or ESP today that could match her cunning, her wisdom, and her expanded way of thinking. She refused to be so narrow and dismiss the tremendous possibilities of extrasensory perception.

After my presentation at Chautauqua, I met up with Dr. Mead and we began discussing the issues of the world. We returned to my hotel and the two of us sat in the study and talked until six o'clock the next morning. In the five or six hours that unfolded, I heard her reflections on how the world would evolve in the years to come. Dr. Mead's reflections were dramatic. She said the family as we know it would begin to disintegrate. This seemed at the time to be a bizarre remark. She elaborated to say that single parent families would become common and the cohesiveness of family life would dwindle. She predicted that divorce would become rampant in our society and children of unmarried mothers would proliferate. At the time, I simply nodded my head. Who would argue with the master? Who would contradict someone who carried a huge rod given to her by pygmies in a small African village? I didn't totally agree, however. I thought that she was probably on the right track but exaggerating to make a point. She felt that the ties, trust and cohesiveness of relationships would weaken and that the collapse of the family would be a prelude to this sad set of circumstances.

The conversation then moved to the effect drugs have on society. Dr. Mead was an advocate of legalizing marijuana, and had strong feelings that drugs would become so high priced on the black market that they would become one of the major destructive forces in our society. This fascinated me as I remembered a conversation I had a decade earlier with a member of the CIA. The CIA agent confided in me that one of Fidel Castro's ambitions was to flood the United States with drugs in order to break down its very fiber and weaken the very core of our society.

As the conversation drifted to crime in general, Dr. Mead predicted that the criminal element would become out of control. She predicted that violence would engulf all ages, not simply the adult domain, and that crime would reach such a destructive point that man would start to isolate himself from the people around him - building homes that resembled prisons to protect himself from the outside world. As the years unfolded, I was reminded of this prediction time and again. Driving down the streets in Los Angeles, seeing bars on the windows and doors is commonplace. In San Juan, Puerto Rico, I visited a friend and his home had a jail cell door that slide back into the wall to reveal the front door. I have met the designer of that cell door, and he has begun installing them across the United States mainland.

Dr. Mead also warned of the increase in terrorism into our once sheltered country. With the World Trade Center bombing and the Oklahoma City bombing, it is obvious that Dr. Mead was right. As a final thought, Dr. Mead predicted that the next change in

American society would be after the turn of the century, and these terrible trends would reverse themselves. As we approach the new millennium, I hope that her brilliant prophecies, which have been eerily accurate, will achieve a 100% success rate and the trends in crime, violence, and breakdown of the family will, in fact, reverse themselves.

Since that dramatic night, and the hours Dr. Mead spent graphically describing her vision of the future, there has rarely been a day when I haven't picked up a newspaper or watched a story on the evening news without thinking about the most remarkable prophet that I have ever met. Don't tell me that no one can foretell the future.

It's hard to believe that thirty years have gone by since that reflective evening, as the events are so clearly impressed upon my memory. The memories of that night often make me wonder what Dr. Mead would think of the changes in society today. As an example, I can't help but feel that she would have very strong feelings about the impact of computers on the lifestyles of today. I suspect that she would feel, as I do, that computers are becoming a potentially damaging force, especially on the emotional and psychological development of children. I am not ignoring advances in favor of comfortable traditions, as I would be by refusing to accept the automobile because of how effective horses were in transportation for so many years. My fears are based on the time children spend in front of a box. Children would rather stay in their rooms, and play games with their friends over the Internet, instead of walking down the street and actually playing with their peers. Isn't it bad enough that we each have a television set in our homes to suck the life and social interactions out of our daily relationships? There was a time when we would sit on the porch to breathe the fresh air and socialize with those on our block. I suggest that that social interaction, done outside with the trees rustling and the wind slowly blowing, is far more productive, healthy, and nurturing than the machine based isolation that TV and computers create. Is the child really learning to feel, touch and communicate with others when he spends hours on end in front of a push-button machine? Today's child spends huge amounts of time in front of the computer, and of the time that is left he divides it between the television and the telephone.

Of course, controlling the amount of time a child spends with various mechanized tools requires the ability of a parent to say "no." It may well be that the average western world parent is beginning to sense that they are losing the capacity to really protect their children due to the accessibility children have to information and graphic exposition available on the Internet and on television. The ratings on movies and the corresponding age limitations to enter movie theaters have some, if very little, effect. However, television and record ratings are going to have no impact at all.

As I travel the western world and listen to parents I get the impression that they feel a helplessness. In different ways they seem to be expressing the opinion that they are having less and less control on how their children turn out. I have heard over and over from parents that no matter how much effort they put into working for the success and maturity of their kids, how the children actually turn out is nothing more than a crapshoot. I believe that a lot of the troubles lie in the parent's chaotic schedule. Parents are working harder and harder to make ends meet and the children are offered less and less interaction time with their parents. As such, the schools and the media are having a greater and greater impact on how our children develop.

There was a time, not all that long ago, when children were not left at home to eat a microwave dinner in front of the television. Even when Mom and Dad had to be away, they made sure that their children were fed a proper dinner at the neighbor's home. There was a time not long ago that everyone knew their neighbors, even in apartment buildings. On rainy days, I looked forward to going to the third floor of my apartment building and playing board games in the hallway with friends.

There is no question that we have to educate our children about sexual activities, the rampant social diseases, and the predators on the street who may invade their personal lives by polluting their minds by selling or sharing questionable material. However, by making these fears so prevalent and pronounced, are we not stripping away a child's right to innocence - his right to feel secure?

Dr. Mead was accurate when she stated that her greatest fear was the disintegration of the family. On a positive note, however, she predicted that this trend would reverse itself after the turn of the century and now that the new millennium is upon us, bright roads may lie ahead. While society today doesn't seem to be able to raise happy, well-adjusted children and the extended family that offered support and guidance in the past is non-existent, Dr. Mead saw something in our future that would indicate a shift back to the close-knit, supportive family. The shift may be brought on by a monumental tragedy, whether it be terrorism, an act of nature, or some other calamity. It has been shown that in times of war and tragedy, people are capable of rising to their highest levels of strength and courage, as well as being able to work and think as a unit for the benefit of all those that are important to them. During these trying times, people stop concentrating simply on the selfish me, myself and 1, and look to how they can better those around them.

It is my belief, prediction and conviction that it will be a "Major Tragedy" that will be the impetus to bring the family, and society, back together. Further still, it is my belief and prediction that the tragedy will not be generated by Mother Nature.

Entertainment

TOM HANKS

Tom Hanks rose to show business fame in a television sitcom named Bosom Buddies. He became one of the few television comics to make the successful transition to movies when he starred in Big. He became an even rarer commodity when he became successful as a serious actor. There is no denying that he is one of the most talented and successful actors working, as his back to back Oscar awards can attest. (For Forrest Gump and *Philadelphia) We* spoke to Tom about working with Steven Spielberg (Saving Private *Ryan) and* the movie industry in general.

Q: How was working with Spielberg?

A: He is a genius.

Q: Any chance of you doing a Bosom Buddy reunion show?

A: I don't think there would be any interest, why?

Q: Just wondering. Do you still dress in women's clothes for reminiscing sake?

A: No, but I do try to sneak into women's dorms.

Q: What do you think will be the most successful type of films in the next millennium?

A: How do you judge success?

Q: Well, first financially and then at Oscar time.

A: Titanic showed that a film can be both, but I think the event films will still be successful financially. It's encouraging that the public is showing their maturity and supporting films that have some deeper application than special effects.

Q: What about Oscar success?

A: Quality films prove successful at the Oscars, it's that simple.

Q: What made Forrest Gump so successful? Was it the special effects, your name...

A: The special effects helped at the box office, it generated publicity. But the last fifteen minutes of the film won the Oscars. No special effects, just heartfelt emotion that the public was able to empathize with.

Reflections on Tom Hanks

There is something uncanny about Tom Hanks. He seems to have a warmth and naturalness that builds a trust between him and his viewers. It is the same trust we had for Humphrey Bogart and Cary Grant. He is able to use that honesty and trust to bring terrific pictures to the screen. Tom seemed to predict a maturity of the movie-going public. He feels that Forrest Gump was successful because of the drama and emotion of the last fifteen minutes. It is my prediction that by the turn of the century, the public will have become saturated with special effects, noise, explosions and fast moving cars. There will be a re-discovery that brilliant films can be made where the most dramatic moments are between personalities and the only noise heard is beautiful background music. The days of Katherine Hepburn and Spencer Tracy, and Humphrey Bogart and Ingrid Bergman will find their way back. There are trends in all areas of show business, and when this more meaningful film genre returns it will be a refreshing discovery for many.

ALICIA SILVERSTONE -- Actress

We ran into Alicia Silverstone at the premier of her made-for-cable movie, *Wildlife Vet*. She made the movie to support one of her favorite charities, International Wildlife Veterinary Services. The premier itself was a benefit for the charity. Being one of the most successful female actors working today, we thought Alicia might be in a unique position to give us some insight and predictions into trends in the movie industry. Specifically, we were interested in her views regarding movie budgets, as she has worked in both big budget films, *Batman & Robin,* and low budget films, Excess Baggage.

Q: Do you think studios will keep making huge budget action movies, now that many of them seem to be losing money?

A: Titanic did good. It depends on the movie - a lot of big budget films still make money.

Q: But with independent films, like *The Full Monty,* making huge money and being made so cheaply, do you think major studios might start saving money and making smaller films?

A: No, they'll still make big event movies. There is room for everything.

Alicia felt confident that the major studios would continue to make huge budget "event movies." She felt that smaller films, even those that are highly successful, wouldn't influence the studios significantly. While a smaller budget movie provides less risk, and the upside seems to be almost unlimited these days, she feels that with the price of the major actors today (over 20 million dollars) large budget films will always have their place in our hometown theaters.

Reflections on Alicia Silverstone

Alicia Silverstone, unquestionably, is one of the hottest female actors working today. We were first introduced to her when she appeared in MTV videos for the rock band Aerosmith. She then starred in her first film, The Crush. Her breakthrough came in her starring role in the movie *Clueless,* which was a huge hit. She has since starred in a number of films including the last installment of *Batman,* where she played BatGirl.

I often think that today it is more difficult for an actor or actress in the movie business than it was in years past. In a bygone era when artists were signed to a specific studio, like MGM, Warner Brothers or Twentieth Century, scripts were written with a particular actor in mind and the studio cared for the handling of the artist. Everything from publicity to accommodations were done with great care. Today, after a movie has been made, the manager or agent of the star has to begin search anew for a project. It is a different ball game now, and there is something to be said for the old time star system.

JERRY SEINFELD

They say that there is nothing more gratifying than retiring on top, and Jerry Seinfeld certainly tested that theory last year. As the star of the top rated television show, *Seinfeld,* Jerry called it quits. The final episode grabbed the nation's attention and became a huge event. The cast of the show graced the cover of hundreds of magazines, there were constant stories in both the print media and broadcast media, and the rumors as to the plot of the final episode ran rampant over the Internet and at water coolers around the country. Jerry did quit, and he did so in the same year he became the highest paid entertainer in the nation, at over $225 million in earnings for the year, far outdistancing such notables as Titanic director James Cameron ($115 million) and media mogul Steven Spielberg ($175 million).

After he left Seinfeld, Jerry made plans to appear on Broadway. He rehearsed for his Broadway appearance at the Comedy and Magic Club in Hermosa Beach, California, where we caught up with him.

Q: Do you like any of the sitcoms on right now?

A: I don't watch too much.

Q: Do you think stand-up comedians will continue to get shows?

A: If they're funny. People act like the networks walk down the street and if you introduce yourself as a stand up you will be given a show. It's not like that. If the comedian is funny, has a decent idea, can write, then the show can be a hit, and studios will keep using them. It's not that you're a stand-up, it's that you have some talent to make people laugh, which is what comedy programs are all about.

Q: The trend seems to be that networks are losing viewers to cable, satellite the networks can continue to be successful?

A: The networks will do fine. They have to compete with the new markets, but if the shows are funny, or quality, or entertaining, they will do fine. Their overall market will shrink, but the hit shows will always draw.

Jerry obviously feels that quality talent can make quality television programming. He did predict that stand-up comedians would still get shows -- he just added the caveat that they must be talented stand-ups. He also predicted the networks would hold their own, maybe losing overall market share, but still packing them in for hit shows and special events, such as the Super Bowl.

Reflections on Jerry Seinfeld

There is no question that one does not have to be a prophet to realize that hit shows will always draw. However, in the future it will be harder to find them with nearly 500 channels to choose from. There may be new techniques to attract viewers to a show -- the promise that the host is going to jump off a building, commit suicide, or mow down a group of lawyers on Wall Street. But it is going to be interesting to see the pollution coming over the airwaves in the form of television programming in the coming years. I think the timing for Seinfeld to call it quits was perfect. He was on the top and able to leave without succumbing to the future's sensationalism. I am afraid that in the future some very important shows will be lost in the shuffle. It may take the old fashioned ballyhoo that was used in the circus days of P.T. Barnum to attract viewers.

HOWARD STERN - radio

Thank God for Kreskin. I know why they call him Amazing -- he has amazing balls the size of an elephant. Here you go Kreskin -- more work from us for free for your new book. I predict that:

1. I feel the Internet will play a big part in the field of entertainment.

2. I predict Magic Johnson will have a sex change operation and replace Sally Jesse Raphael.

3. I predict the morals of this country will become looser and relaxed.

4. I predict there will be no more FCC in the new millennium.

5. I predict Gary DellAbate will get a live television show where he will show his testicles one day a week.

6. I predict you, Kreskin, will be locked up in a mental institution and carted away in the new millennium.

7. I also predict that everyone will develop the ability to read thoughts and make tables rattle and Kreskin will be out of work in the next millennium.

That is my answer.
Yours in the next millennium,
Howard Stern, King of all Media

P.S. I predict you will shake hands so hard with a biker that he will beat the crap out of you.

(Knowing how bizarre Howard handles his presentations, it should be said that Howard gave these predictions, live, during his radio program)

Reflections on Howard Stern

I am constantly asked what Howard Stern is really like and I find the question rather amusing. I find it amusing because I assume that anyone that regularly listens to him would see "through" his caustic image and see the real Stern. He happens to be a rather conservative individual! He is extraordinarily family oriented and very protective over his private life and those in it. Beyond the facade of humor and outrage is an incredibly brilliant man who has kept his values intact throughout his successful career. I can't imagine anyone who has ever worked for him not to espouse the loyalty that is ingrained in his work ethic. All the praise aside, there is no question that he is outrageous.

I have always enjoyed appearing on his radio and television programs. One standout memory was the two hours I spent on the air with him in October of 1997. My appearance resulted in a dramatic live seance in which tables were held down by participants in the studio. It was not a trick or a stage illusion. There were no stooges involved. I have always maintained that what I do has a tremendous amount of legitimacy to it. Through the concentration and energy of the individuals in the studio that day, all strangers to me, we created a damn exciting happening.

I found it refreshing the way Howard handled my request for a contribution to this book. He decided to do it on the air and kept in character. How could we not relate to some of his prophecies?

I cannot avoid commenting, here in passing, on some of the critics of Howard Stern. I find it fascinating that individuals will devote such a tremendous amount of time in their life listening to hour after hour of Stern broadcasts and then sit down and write the

Federal Communications Commission attacking Stern's program as damaging to the public interest. I find it difficult to understand how these "authorities" presume to be above the deleterious effects of Stern. Aren't they afraid that if they are listening day after day they are going to be harmed in some way or are they above the people they are protecting? Are they wiser and holier than thou? Censorship has always intrigued me as heinous. There are always those who are able to sample that which they wish to sensor. Herein lies the monumental hypocrisy. 1, for one, find Howard Stern to be the best social critic/satirist since Mark Twain and Oscar Wilde. It is interesting to note that Mark Twain was censored many times in his life, and his writings were banned on many occasions.

With all the kindness and enthusiasm Stern has expressed for my work, he knows without having to be a thought reader that I do feel a bit queasy when he sees me on the air and says, "Oh, Kreskin, about the size of your..."

ROSEANNE

As one of the most influential women in entertainment, Roseanne has been at the top of the headlines for years. She retired from her top rated television sitcom and now hosts her own daytime talk show. We took this opportunity to ask her about television talk shows.

Q: Who will be around in the TV talk wars in the next millennium?

A: Dave, Jay, Oprah and me.

Q: Can you win your time slot?

A: We've got a great show. We'll have to perfect it, but we should do good.

Q: Do you think Dave can ever top Jay in the ratings again?

A: Who the f*** knows.

Q: No one, just asking your opinion.

A: I'm just worrying about my show.

Q: In the next millennium what will be the main TV delivery mechanism?

A: Are you on drugs?

Q: I'm talking about broadcast, cable, satellite....
A: Don't forget telephone cable, and internet stuff.
Q: What do you think will end up winning?
A: Ask an electrician.
Q: Can I have a kiss?
A: Make an appointment with my dog.

Reflections on Roseanne

I have never personally met Roseanne, but she is obviously always fun to talk to and will not disappoint any interviewer. While she is obviously not a prophet, she is a tremendous wit and a sharp gal. I thought she was very honest when she commented that while she has a great show, she will have to perfect it. She is willing to admit that it may need some alterations and refinements. As for her prediction about talk shows, I don't think there is much doubt that David Letterman, Jay Leno and Oprah Winfrey will be successful into the next millennium. If Roseanne's television show falls by the wayside, I have a strong feeling her resourcefulness and ingenuity will bring her other avenues of success in television. She is not to be ignored.

BURT REYNOLDS

In the movie industry, it is tough to find someone as successful for as long as Burt Reynolds. He began starring in films in the 1960's and has worked continuously since then, culminating recently with an Oscar nomination for his role in "Boogie Nights." We spoke with this legendary actor about the movie business and his thoughts on his career.

Q: Do you see any major trends in the movie business?

A: Yea, I'm getting more roles.

Q: In general though, any changes in the industry?

A: It's a weird business, there are no trends.

Q: Do you think you might win an Oscar in the coming years?

A: That's not up to me. I just go to work.

Q: Who's going to be the next big director?

A: What's up with these questions?

Q: Just curious.

Reflections on Burt Reynolds

Burt's prediction was in the negative, that there are no real trends in a business as disjointed and unpredictable as the movie business. On the contrary, I find the business to be replete with trends. There were periods of time when musicals were at the top. Both westerns and horror movies have also been trendy and successful at times. However, Burt was happy with his recent popularity and predicted he would continue to receive many offers. It is remarkable to see Reynold's ability to bounce back after some lean years in which he nearly disappeared from the industry. I always enjoyed working with him. He was an easy read -- very open. He was always very comfortable to work with and had a quiet sense of humor. He had a habit of sneaking up behind me and saying my name. I would turn around and see him standing there, in an unassuming position, smiling as only Burt Reynolds can do.

ROGER EBERT - Movie Critic

Within the next 1,000 years, the "feelies" of science fiction will become a reality, and movies will take place entirely in our heads. The computerized technology will be able to directly access and control those brain zones dealing with the five senses, as well as with pleasure and thought. The alternative worlds of these fantasies will become so addictive that opium dens will pale by comparison and "moviegoers" will be separated from their alternative lives only reluctantly. The human race will gradually die out, as fantasy becomes easier, more pleasant and safer than dealing with real life. The last surviving human will die with a smile at a very old age, still plugged in and enjoying great sex.

Reflections on Roger Ebert

Roger Ebert is a legend. He is a hugely successful movie critic and co-host of the fascinating weekly movie review show, Siskel and Ebert. His insightful and truly compassionate reviews are unique. I enjoy his commentary on classic movies as well as current releases and I was delighted Ebert submitted his reflections on the movies of the next millennium. His predictions are certainly very futuristic thoughts. The concept that movies will take place entirely inside our heads seems incredible. While it might seem impossible, is it truly beyond the capacity of man? The respected Psychiatrist Dr. Gerard Sunnen has remarked that the nervous system may be tapped into human physiology and the brain can influence the process. So, perhaps Ebert's speculation will become a dramatic reality sooner than we think.

Ebert also speculates on the downside of experiencing these alternate lives. I love his final reflection -- not that there will be one final surviving human -- but that the extreme impact of these fantasy experiences might cause man to find it very difficult to separate himself from the fantasy and return to true reality. I wonder if Ebert is being a little sarcastic in an effort to get across an important message -- that no matter how sophisticated the technology will be in the next millennium, man will have to keep his feet grounded and live in reality at least some of the time. With the common predictions that movies will be able to be requested and started in a matter of seconds, from home, there is no doubt that the fantasy world could become addictive. It is a most interesting reflection. Thank goodness Ebert couched his comments with a touch of humor. It is the same sophistication he uses in his commentaries on Siskel and Ebert.

WILLIAM SHATNER

In the next 1,000 years, the playgoers will not come to the play, the play will go to the audience in Holo-Decks in every home. Three-dimensional images of the actors will perform in your living room - sitting in your chair, eating at your tables, yes, even drinking your beer. They will speak to you personally, call you by name, share some of your most intimate thoughts - yes, even erotic ones. You'll smell them. You'll feel them. You might even taste them. Think of the immediacy of any dramatic situation. Talk about slipping on a banana peel, you'll feel the thud as the body hits the floor!

Reflections on William Shatner

I met Bill Shatner nearly thirty years ago when he was a guest on my international television series, The Amazing World of Kreskin. Shatner flew out to Canada where we taped and he enjoyed his experience so much that he asked to return. Shatner ended up doing a total of four appearances on my show. His appearances were always special, but one stands out in my mind.

Nothing was ever pre-arranged on my show - the guest never quite knew what to expect. When Shatner arrived in Canada he was driven to a local bookstore. He was told to go in the store and purchase three books. He was instructed to tell no one which books he bought, especially me. When he approached the bookstore he noticed that there was a sign on the door that read "Closed." Shatner knocked on the door, and the owner who was closing up looked over to the door and began to point at the sign on the door. I can only imagine his surprise when he saw the familiar face of William Shatner! The owner immediately opened the door and invited Shatner in. Shatner explained that he wanted three books. The owner asked him which three and was surprised when Shatner said it didn't matter. Shatner bought three books and proceeded to the television studio. When he came on my program he still had the books wrapped in the original paper. I asked him to take one out of his choosing, turn to a page and begin reading to himself. As he did, I described a scene with a knife in a person's back. Shatner was amazed. He was reading from a murder mystery and the exact sentence he was reading to himself was identical to the scene I had just described to the audience.

Shatner has a fascination with the unknown. He has even written a novel about Houdini and Conan Doyle. Additionally, Shatner starred in the Star Trek television show and movies, which projected ideas of futuristic developments. So, with those experiences in mind it is interesting to examine Shatner's projections for the next millennium. They sound highly futuristic and somewhat with a tone of science fiction, but when we look back at what has been accomplished in the last fifty years we can only wonder if his predictions might come true. If they did, how would we react to watching a hologram play in our own homes where we see, feel, smell and touch the experience? Can you imagine feeling the thud of a body as it his the floor?

JERRY SPRINGER - Talk Show Host

Jerry Springer is the talk show bad boy. His talk show burst on to the scene with topics and guests that had never been seen before. His guests commonly got into fistfights and swearing matches on the air. The show often included nudity and racy topics. His show began beating Oprah. Amid accusations that his guests were actors and that the fighting was getting out of hand, he toned his show down, refusing to let guests fight any longer. We asked him about his show and the future of talk.

Q: Will your show be at the top in the next millennium?

A: I hope to be alive in the next millennium, I'll worry about the show later.

Q: Seriously.

A: The show has a huge following. If we keep creating the entertainment, people will continue to watch.

Q: Can you beat Oprah without the fighting?

A: We create fun shows. People relate and our ratings reflect that. We can beat Oprah.

Jerry predicts he can last into the next millennium and that he can beat Oprah in the ratings -- even without the fighting on his program. The question is what is more popular -- the high road, or the low road.

Reflections on Jerry Springer

As of this time, Springer has toned down his no fighting policy. The fistfights have begun to return to his show, as the morality of television seems to be in the ratings. While the powers that be stood on ethics and demanded the show remove fighting from the format, they quickly changed their tune when the ratings dropped. Their ethical position shifted, as money was the governing factor. After all, the Jerry Springer Show is a business, and it has been an extremely successful business.

While there have been accusations that the people appearing on the show are actors, the truth is it doesn't matter. When a non-actor appears on television, he appears with years of rehearsal training found in watching television. The guest knows both consciously and unconsciously what is expected of him and how to act. They take on the role that has been predefined by the show, and whether or not they are paid performers matters not. Remember Shakespeare once said, "the world is a stage and we are the actors upon it."

To see this effect in action, watch a talk show closely. If you watch the guest's eyes carefully, you will invariably notice them glancing off to the side to see the monitors. The monitors show what will be seen on the television screen. The guest is acutely aware of this and wants to see that they are looking the part. This was something the everyday guest never did in the past. As a result, the fights on the Jerry Springer Show don't have to be staged by the director. The past pattern of guests creates a expectancy in the current guest's mind to act that way. It is similar to what happens in a hypnotism demonstration. The subject knows what is expected of him, and he does it. The guests on the Jerry Springer Show might be actors, but they are natural actors -- the same kind that can be found on every street corner throughout our society. You, my dear reader, might be one of them.

ROGER AILES - Chairman, CEO, Fox News

I've been busy traveling and running a new network. The questions you've asked are difficult to answer and it's anybody's guess. However, my view is that we're moving to a broader and broader choice of programming. Someday you'll walk into the living room, your entire wall will be a television set, and you'll speak to the wall and say, "Call Mom and show me the news without Russia and Bosnia." Through voice data, the next thing that will happen is your mother will appear on the wall via video phone, while your video retainer edits the news to your liking and then plays it back for you while you change clothes to go out jogging.

That's one vision of the future. Arguably the companies best positioned for the future are:
Microsoft, particularly if they end up buying NBC. (I believe GE will eventually get out of the television business by selling NBC.)
ABC because of their vertical integration with Disney programming.
News Corp. – Rupert Murdoch's company because it has the most worldwide reach and has broadcast, cable, Internet and international distribution.
Time Warner/CNN because they have both news and programming capability with current world-wide distribution.

A few networks will exist, but they will be more like programming services and people will set-up their television seasons the same way advertisers do now. They will select those shows they think will be hits and program their season so that their set automatically flips to whatever network program service they want. Loyalty to programmers will not exist, news will not be seen on the broadcast networks with the exception of magazine shows and occasional breaking news. Cable news such as: CNN, MSNBC perhaps, and the FOX News Channel will provide all news -- all the time.
The FOX News Channel, which I'm currently developing, is seen in about thirty-five million homes. Within the next few years it will

be in sixty million homes, equal to CNN. FOX has a younger brand, and draws younger viewers. The current average age of the viewer at CNN is 63. The current average age of the FOX News Channel viewer is about 44 years of age, so I believe that FOX News Channel will bring along the next generation of news viewers. The network business will depend solely on the quality of the program service they provide to a worldwide audience, but the network structure is beginning to breakdown now and will continue to with station affiliates becoming more and more independent.

Reflections on Roger Ailes

To me, the comments of Roger Ailes are monumental in scope. The comments, while they are on the minds of many people in broadcasting and academia, have never been spoken so openly and frankly. In many ways, there is a fear in the industry of facing up to the reality of what is going to happen in television news in the next millennium.

I have been blessed with knowing Roger for over thirty years. Our friendship began when he worked on the Mike Douglas Show. At the time, it was the definitive daytime talk show in the United States. Although I set a record by appearing on the show 118 times, I would visit with Roger even on days I wasn't scheduled to appear. My conversations with him were so vibrant and thought provoking.

Roger helped invent the format for my appearances on the Douglas Show. In the first segment, I would sit with Mike and comment on various issues. The conversations used my expertise as a mentalist and ranged from reading the thoughts of a famous political figure who was about to make a dramatic decision, to the issue of human/animal telepathy.

During the next segment I would perform thought reading experiments with the studio audience. Mike was my aisle man. In the old days of Vaudeville, the aisle man was a partner of the swami who sat on stage. The aisle man would phrase questions that would give clues to the "psychic." We have seen this type of charade exposed many times. Mike was not that type of aisle man. He merely facilitated the communication between the audience and myself. I remember one time Mike asked a studio member if she had ever met me. We were all surprised when she said she had. It turned out that as I arrived for my appearance I passed by the line of audience members waiting to go in to see the show. I said hello to everyone as I entered the studio. That hello was what the woman meant when she said she had met me before. Mike then clarified that beside that hello, she had never met me before, nor had any previous conversations with me. Mike was always very careful and protective of me, as was the entire crew on the show.

For the final segment of my appearance I would perform a dramatic test with the celebrity who was on the Douglas Show that day. On one show, I handed Bette Davis a book and asked her to think of a page number. Once she picked the number, I asked her to turn to that page. When she got to where the page should be, she realized that every page in the book was intact, except the page she just said -- that page had been torn out. I asked Mike to look in his shirt pocket, and he pulled out the missing page Davis had thought of. Davis was so amazed that she interrupted her interview four or five times to say, "that was impossible."

It was this format that Roger Ailes invented and which worked so well. Indeed, when my television series began, this is the format I used for the full 5 1/2 years of the show.

Roger's career after he left the Mike Douglas Show is legendary. He became a counsel and communications representative for President Ronald Reagan and then President George Bush. During the Bush administration, he left politics and returned to broadcasting. This was a tough decision for Roger. I know from his commentary that he went into politics hoping to make constructive changes, however he was frustrated by the difficulty in achieving the ends that even the most idealistic President hopes to. This country is evidently burdened more than ever by an incredible bureaucracy.

His comments about the future of broadcasting are awesome in their scope. Again we see what has been hinted about for years, that few networks will exist in the future. He predicts that the broadcasting of news will leave the networks. This seems accurate

as we currently see the cable news powers becoming more and more encompassing. Additionally, Ailes shares the views we
see in the Regis Philbin and Kathie Lee entries of this book that loyalty to programmers will decrease. Ailes sees that in the future loyalty in the news area will be non-existent.

Finally, I find amazing his opening comments regarding the wall of the room being a giant television screen. As we discuss such options as the ability to ask your television for a particular program, or to dial your Mom for a videoconference we see that what was once merely science fiction is becoming reality. It boggles the mind.

CASEY KASEM - Radio Legend

Dear Kreskin: I received your August 21st letter asking me to discuss radio's "next 1,000 years" for your upcoming new millennium book.

Unfortunately, I haven't a clue as to what the distant or even near-distant future will bring. I'm just carrying my own career in radio forward, planning a few years ahead at a time, and adjusting with whatever happens. So, I'll have to politely decline the offer to pontificate.

Nevertheless, I wish you success with your book.

Yours truly,

Casey Kasem

Reflections on Casey Kasem

It would be hard to imagine that there would be anyone who has not heard Casey Kasem's name during his decades of success. When you think of radio, music, and the presentation of hit records, Kasem is at the top of the list. I got a kick out of his response to my request and I think that he expressed it sincerely.

CHARLES M. SCHULZ - Cartoonist,

Creator of Peanuts

The obvious shrinking of comic strips in the daily and Sunday papers is probably the biggest worry and annoyance of comic strip artists today. Most feel that there seems to be no solution to this and feel robbed of their chance to do better work. In many ways comic strips are funnier than they were in the old days, but they're certainly not drawn as well. We are living in an age dominated by television and those of us who love comic strips feel distressed because our work does not have the impact that the comic strips had years ago. Things move on, of course, and we all have to adapt. Our future simply lies in the hands of subscribing editors.

Reflections on Charles Schulz

During my performances, I have a running challenge. I ask the promoter of my concert to hide my paycheck somewhere in the hall. If I cannot find it, I don't get paid. Thankfully, in over 6000 performances, I have only failed to find the check nine times. A few years ago, I attempted to read the thoughts of the promoter who had hidden my check. I wandered into the audience and ended up approaching a man who had been enjoying the performance. I asked him to move a bit, and it turned out that the man had been sitting on my check. The man was none other than the great Charles Shulz. I was thrilled, as I had been an admirer of Schulz's comic strip, "Peanuts" for most of my life.

Comics have been hugely influential in my life. In my pre-teens I read "Blondie" religiously, and have enjoyed comics ever since. However, the most important impact comics have had on me occurred when I was five. I was given a comic book by a young man. The comic book was "Mandrake the Magician" by Lee Falk. The hero was a mastermind with hypnotic telepathic powers. This comic gave me focus and from that moment on Mandrake dictated my future work and ambitions.

As for Shulz's comments on comics, the observation that comic strips in general are not being drawn as well as in the past really hit home with me. The earlier comics seem to me to be much less confusing. The characters are clear in their ideals and their strengths. The confusion and doubts of mortal man was absent, allowing the characters to have a more pristine image. This image was one to be admired. I miss the comics of the past.

DICK CLARK

In the next millennium our TV will marry our computer. The child of this "shotgun" marriage will be an awesome offspring. It will entertain, inform, order, file and organize our pitiful lives, currently in disarray. We'll have endless choices of material to watch, survey and select. Music and TV programs will come directly into a home device. It will store your choices. No need to hike down to the record outlet. No more video stores. You'll have your favorite film on demand -- when you want it. No need to watch TV when the programs are scheduled. You can order them when you want them. The school library will pop up on your screen, as will your favorite merchandise catalogue. No need to leave the house, just place orders - you'll be billed. The bank will take care of everything. You'll still need some source of income, so perhaps you may have to leave home occasionally.

Whether or not we'll have the time, interest or money to indulge ourselves in these endless choices ... only time will tell.

Reflections on Dick Clark

There cannot be anyone in North America who doesn't know the name of Dick Clark. From the days of hosting American Bandstand when we saw teenagers dancing to the current rock tunes to his hosting New Years Eve from New York City, Clark is a giant in the industry. His legend is as big behind the scenes as it is in front of the camera as he produces many television specials each year, including the American Music Awards. He seems; to have a handle on the appetite of the viewing public. He is often described as the eternally youthful Dick Clark and I cannot imagine he aged more than a couple years since the fifties.

I am delighted that he has given his reflections for this book. Again, we see the almost inevitable reminder that the computer and television will marry. I love him calling it a shotgun marriage, however his comment that the results will be awesome makes me reflect. If you read between the lines, you can see that like the buggy whip, technology will run record and video stores out of business. Additionally, Clark comments that there will be little need to leave the house -everything will be done at home. He conjectures whether or not we will have the time, interest or money to indulge ourselves. I wonder if we will have the interest level with such an endless stimuli of information and entertainment. How long could it be before a state of boredom and dullness sets in. Perhaps in that area, if I can quote Clark, only "time will tell."

FRED DE CORDOVA -- Television Producer

For years, the man behind the success of Johnny Carson and the Tonight Show was Fred de Cordova. As Executive Producer he had input into the show that was second only to Johnny. His career in late night talk puts him in a unique position to comment on the current war between David Letterman and Jay Leno. We met up with Fred at the Entertainment Fellowship Dinner held at CBS studios.

Q: Do you think Jay can stay on top of the ratings indefinitely?

A: Jay puts on an entertaining show, he will always do well.

Q: If CBS increases its primetime ratings, can Letterman get his viewership back up, or is Jay a permanent fixture as the leader?

A: They have different audiences. Jay is more mainstream and will probably stay on top.

Coming from the Tonight Show, Fred might have a little bias towards the man who followed his boss into the coveted Tonight Show hosting chair, but he does predict that Jay will continue his ratings domination over Letterman.

Reflections on Fred De Cordova

As executive producer of *The Tonight Show,* Fred was always a mediator. He was careful never to put the star of the show into a compromising situation. As you can see from his comments, he still has kept to his policy of having nice things to say about everyone. He is truly a diplomat.

Recently I did an appearance on the *Howie Mandel Show.* While I was relaxing in my dressing room I heard a knock on the door. I opened the door and there stood Fred De Cordova. Even though he is in his 80's, I noticed he has a zest, an energy, and a wit so sharp he is probably ready to start *The Tonight Show* all over again. He still consults with NBC and is very active in broadcasting. It is truly a study in the industry to talk to a man who has been so successful as a producer, from *The Jack Benny Show* to Carson's *Tonight Show.* The two of us had a terrific conversation and it reminded me of what a true talent Fred is. His style during *The Tonight Show* tapings was remarkable. He sat behind the camera quietly, rarely standing, rarely speaking. But by just a glance and a few motions, he and Johnny Carson communicated. I don't believe there was any telepathic communication occurring between them, although certainly much of their dialogue was non-verbal. The truth of the matter is that the show was so thoroughly planned and thought out that it ran completely smoothly. The interviews were never practiced, but the guest did go over their topics ahead of time, and Johnny made the stars shine at their best. He was a master at taking an individual and illuminating him. So often today, when you watch talk shows you'll notice that the host will try to get in the funny line and try to be the center of attention. It is as if the host forgets he will be back the next night. Johnny allowed the guest to shine. Johnny's unselfish style made him a huge success. Johnny also had a mid-Western voice that gave him a generic quality, allowing viewers to identify with him as if he was from their own home town, no matter where they were watching. I predict that it will be at least a dozen years before we see a host of the same quality as Johnny Carson -- a person so well read, knowledgeable, and aware of music, politics, and sports, and at the same time so keenly tuned in to human nature as to extract the maximum comedy out of any discussion or scenario. The prediction I just made sounds rather negative, but it is true that I do not see anyone at this moment in time who has the kind of character, scope and talent as Johnny.

There was once an incident on *The Tonight Show* that Fred De Cordova could comment upon, but won't. In order to save the comedian some embarrassment, I won't name him, but he was a top professional. He was booked on *The Tonight Show,* as he had numerous times. He didn't rehearse because his reputation preceded him -- there was no need for a rehearsal. As the interview on the show began to unfold, Johnny suddenly realized that the comedian wasn't as sharp as he once was. Age had finally caught up and took its toll. I could see in watching Johnny a dramatic realization of the change in mental ability of his guest, and Johnny handled it brilliantly. He looked square in the eyes of the guest and asked questions that were nearly rhetorical. Almost every question could be answered with a yes or no. Johnny carried on one of the most challenging interviews he had ever done. Johnny carried both ends of the interview in order to save the stature of his guest. I know Fred would call that "top professionalism."

CHUCK JONES -- Animator of Bugs Bunny

As the animator of Bugs Bunny, Chuck Jones is one of the most popular cartoon artists of all time. His work hangs in galleries and in private collections around the world. We asked Chuck about emerging trends in animation.

Q: What do you think will be the popularity of cartoons in the next millennium?

A: Kids always love cartoons. They will continue to boom.

Q: Do you see more or less animated feature films in the next century?

A: There are quite a bit now. It is interesting to see animation aimed at older audiences, like Beavis & Butthead, and Southpark.

Q: What will be the big animated hits in the next millennium?

A: Disney will always do well. It's tough to say.

Reflections on Chuck Jones

It is a source of fascination to me that cartoons have become so popular with adults. It may be the trend of the future due to technological advances. It may become "easier" to create cartoons than to hire actors and actresses, build sets, creating lighting, and go on location to film in live action. It would be a rather intriguing development if cartoons would begin to replace living images on television. We would only hear the performer's voice. I wonder how Walt Disney would feel about the innovations taking place in animated cartoons these days.

Chuck felt confident that cartoons would certainly have a place as entertainment for kids in the next millennium. He felt the more interesting issue was the popularity of cartoons with adults. He predicted that Disney would maintain its dominance in the animated feature film genre, even with strong challengers such as DreamWorks.

I find that the Disney cartoons are still rich in my memory. My two favorites are Snow White and the Seven Dwarfs, and Pinocchio. In Snow White there were some ominous, frightening scenes with the wicked witch. It is my prediction that with the increase in the adult audience for cartoons, the next millennium will see a major horror cartoon developed that could become so successful it may receive a special award.

JOHN GAMBLING - WOR Broadcaster

After appearing on John Gambling's morning program, I interviewed him on the future of radio.

Q: In talk radio, what do you think is going to be the situation in the next Millennium? Do you think there are going to be striking changes?

A: I think talk radio will probably continue to grow. Like everything else in life, radio moves in cycles. Talk radio was gone for a while, and now it is back again, stronger than ever. I think it will continue to get even stronger because I think more and more of us will have information laid upon us by satellite, cable, cell phones and pagers. One of the great things about talk radio is companionship. As we become more isolated as individuals, and we are, we will become more isolated in our own little world. Talk radio is a wonderful way for people to connect with other people -- whether it is a talk show host or other callers. It makes you feel good and I think what is going to happen is that you will find that people listen to hosts because we validate other people's own beings, their own morals, ethics, thoughts and life styles. I think what will happen is life styles will begin to diverge even further and you will find more talk radio.

Q: You said something and it is a theme I have found in 20 some interviews -- that we are going to become isolated at some time.

A: Yes. I think so and we see the trend happening every day.

Q: John, you have a history of three generations of broadcasting. How do you see yourself in the New Millennium? Do you see yourself busy as ever?

A: Yes, but I don't see myself doing what I do now - "Rambling with Gambling" -- forever.

Q: You don't?

A: No. Absolutely not. I want some day to do something different from what I do now. The reason I want to do something different is not because I don't like what I do -- I love what I do -- but I have a desire and a love to make things and I want to make something -- manufacture something. I want to be involved in a business that actually makes something that you can touch, feel or hold -- not something that is ethereal. Not something that goes out and disappears forever. Even though on AM radio it literally goes on forever. The sound of my voice goes into space and because of the radio signals, it travels to who knows how far.

Q: Does that give you a strange feeling sometimes?

A: I don't think about it much, but if you think about it, it will wack you that possibly on another planet, a hundred billion light years from here, some day they will hear not only me, but hear my grandfather and my father before me, because it just continues to go on and on.

Q: I could just hear your grandfather singing "Pack Up All Your Troubles." You've, of course, heard that.

A: Oh, I heard that many times.

Q: What year do you think a female will become President of the United States?

A: I am going to say -- 2012.

Q: What do you think is going to be the height of man in the next millennium?

A: About 6' 1", on average.

Q: What do you think a loaf of bread will cost by the year 3000?

A: $3,000.

Q: Who do you think is going to be remembered as one of the great mind's in this century?

A: Great minds, that's difficult. There aren't too many people who fall into a "great mind" category. There are politicians that I think of, and Billy Graham comes to my mind, but he is not a great mind, he is a great spiritualist. He is a wonderful man, but I don't think that is what you are looking for.

Q: I would pick Churchill.

A: Well you see, Churchill -- that goes back a while -- I am not familiar enough with him. In the last 50 years, however, it might be hard to pick someone.

Reflections on John Gambling

The Gamblings have been a part of my life since day one. The radio show, "Rambling with Gambling" on WOR goes back three generations. All of the shows have been done live and they have run from two to four hours each morning, five days a week. They have been a staple on the radio dial forever. One of my favorite childhood experiences was listening to the original Gambling announcing the closed schools during snowstorms. Everyone would sit riveted to the radio hoping that their school was mentioned. There is something to be said about awakening every morning and hearing a reassuring and familiar voice. The Gamblings have been on the radio for as long as I have listened and they are as familiar a voice as many a family member.

John is a very down-to-earth man. He has few illusions of having some grand place in the world. As important as he is to the radio station he works for, he has a casual unassuming quality. He clearly realizes that once the radio is turned off, listeners return to their lives, dealing with problems, challenges and loves. He enjoys radio, but at the same time he doesn't overestimate its importance. I find fascinating his desire to enter a field where he can make something that can actually be touched, felt and held. He compares this desire to his current profession where his "product," his voice, is ethereal. It goes out over the airways and "disappears forever." His interest in "creating" demonstrates a quality about his personality that is uplifting and genuine. While his broadcasts seem to disappear as soon as they are heard, he does mention the concept that the sound waves travel like light into space. That is a strange, almost mystical, thought. Somehow, I can see and hear Rod Serling embracing the concept in the Twilight Zone.

DAN WALDRON - TV Commercial Producer

Television commercials are creatures of fads. The fads are of two kinds: what is current in the big world outside of TV, the world of popular culture; and, what is current in the style of TV commercial making itself.

The first kind of fad -- dealing with popular culture -- shows up in TV commercials in the settings, wardrobe and language used. They reflect whatever is current and whatever is politically correct. In a less tangible way this kind of fad also comes through in its psychological stance.

A prediction into the next millennium regarding his kind of fad would have to be general: whatever fad crops up, they'll be reflected in the TV commercials. It will also be reflected in any type of advertising the future may see, as television as we know it may undergo drastic changes in time.

The second type of fad -- that of TV commercial style -- is even harder to predict. Right now, at this very moment, the TV tube is awash with commercials that have a saturated look. To the eye they appear underexposed. This is a stylistic device and will fade away when a new novelty of style comes along. TV commercials at present are heavy on music and humor. In the advertising world this is known as "soft sell." The pitchman of old has nearly vanished from the tube. Another stylistic device is the use of key words with, or between, scenes. Still another stylistic device is the use of quick cuts, although this has moderated a great deal after a few years of frantic shotgunning of images. Ever-refreshing style is one way to attract attention, which is what TV commercial are all about.

An honest prediction for the next millennium can only be that styles of commercial-making will continue to evolve. If the pace of life picks up further, then these styles will come and go more quickly.

Overall comments:

We are in a culture of images. Words are replaced with symbols. Ironically, we are harking back to a pre-writing civilization. Literature tends to be either exceedingly long or exceedingly short. We have either an endless novel by John Irving, or the USA Today which offers us the printed version of the TV sound bite. Will we ever arrive at a happy medium? I doubt it.

MTV has been responsible for much of the frenetic nature of recent TV commercials, and by extension, all advertising and the media that carries advertising. There are two observations to be made about MTV. One is that its character is that of a mosaic. We get the big picture only through the presentation of many small images. Second, people who control advertising today -- corporations and businesses with products to sell -- have as their advertising managers and often their CEOs, people who were raised on MTV. The older generation is dwindling fast. That generation might watch Lawrence Welk re-runs on PBS, but it doesn't buy products. Therefore, it doesn't count, at least not in the eyes of the product sellers. So, the TV commercials are aimed at the younger crowd who understand, and open their wallets, to the visual and spoken stimuli presented MTV style on the screen.

Incidentally, it is a misapprehension to think that advertising agencies are wholly responsible for the content and style of TV commercials. They are only reacting to the instructions they've been given by their clients -- the corporate guys who say "yes" or "no" to the commercials. It is true that these instructions are turned into the crazy form we see on TV because most ad agency copywriters and art directors are young. But so are their client counterparts.

Predicting anything as volatile as TV commercials is a hopeless task, especially if "predicting" means being specific about what will happen during the next thousand years. For the short run, however, I predict that TV commercials will continue as they are for as long as the economy stays good. If there is a serious downturn, such as a recession or depression, we can expect to see the return of the hard sell -- commercials that deal more directly with the product. There will be fewer commercials like the one where the Chevy Blazer goes through nature's obstacle course, with rolling logs, falling rocks, and animals running wild. If times got tough, such commercials would have a lot of spoken words and they'd all deal with features of the vehicles, instead of visual, indirect messages.

The use of music and humor is much more valuable than most clients ever know, because they hook people. They make them watch, and, more importantly, make them WANT to watch. If watching a commercial is a pleasant experience, even a truly amusing one, you'll watch. Take the Taco Bell dog commercials as an example.

TV commercial making is a branch of the film industry. It's all technology. Today, film is being replaced by videotape, or some form of digital reproduction. The effects that can be achieved by the manipulation of electronics are practically endless. They are limited only by budgets. When you can show Fred Aster dancing with a vacuum cleaner or John Wayne holding a bottle of beer, both simply clever manipulations of old and newly shot resources, you can do just about any sleight-of-hand. To me, this is video-porn, but to others, apparently, it is fascinating, if not memorable.

Is it possible that in a thousand years there won't even be television. There may not even be Earth. Who knows what there will be. Will there be manufacturers? Products? Customers? To predict intelligently we have to assume everything will change. We can't speak wisely based on the way things are now. Who in his right mind a thousand years ago would have predicted pictures moving through the air or vehicles that move themselves or aircraft that could fly across the oceans in mere hours? We must believe that the future holds things we cannot now imagine.

However, let's look at some wild imaginings about TV commercials anyway:

1.   You'll get a little tiny device that's free. You can insert it into your TV set and it will run a minute of entertainment in which a product is incidentally advertised.

2.   You'll get a tiny device you can put in your ear and a whole program and/or TV commercial can be played with sound and pictures in your brain.

3.   Individuals can't buy TV Sets. You'll get a device when you're born that will receive whatever anyone wants to send.

4.   TV commercials will take on a "virtual reality" function, so that you can participate. For example, you can individualize the commercial for a pain remedy like Tylenol so it advertises in terms of whatever pain you have.

5.   3-D, combined with holograms and video projection, will give you life-size fully-dimensional images right in your home.

6.   New technology will make it possible to try the product being advertised, here and now. For example, a commercial for the candy bar Snickers would let you reach for a Snickers and try it.

Reflections on Dan WALDRON

Dan WALDRON and I hold a mutual interest in the history of the great performers and the art of conjuring. WALDRON is a connoisseur of the great Harry Blackstone, Sr. Blackstone, who was called the Great Illusionist, traveled the United States throughout the 1950's doing a full evening old fashioned magic show. Waldron is an encyclopedia of knowledge on Blackstone, as well as other legendary performers.

Until recently I hadn't realized that the "retired" Dan Waldron was a major producer of television commercials. His credits include some of the top automobile commercials of recent years. I consider his entry on commercials one of the gems of this book. When I first received it I wanted to run out and share it with psychology professors, teachers of advertising, sociologists, and communicators. There is much to be understood beyond the mere commercial, yet the power of commercials cannot be underestimated. Billions of dollars are spent on, and as a result of, commercials. His entry is absolutely riveting and worth reflecting on.

JOHN F. VORISEK - Sound Enterprises

Less than fifty years ago, the average moviegoer went to his or her neighborhood motion picture theater and was offered a single screen with a single choice of presentation. The film was projected on a screen whose dimensions were a ratio of 4 wide by 3 high. The film was normally black and white and the sound was monorail with the highest frequency being 6,500 cycles. By today's standards, 6,500 cycles is quite low in fidelity.

Today, it is not unusual for the normal theater to be a multiplex, with fifteen or more screens, each offering a different wide-screen film, almost always in color, with digital, stereophonic sound with a minimum of six discreet sound tracks.

In addition, you might choose to see a film six months later, in your home, via video tape, cable or satellite. You can view these videos on a forty-plus inch television screen offering many discreet, digital stereo sound tracks.

During the next ten years, the multiplex theaters will be replaced with entertainment complexes that will offer giant screens, three dimensional movies, and pictures with unbelievable clarity, brightness and color. And these films will be transmitted to the theater by satellite and projected by laser systems.

In addition to theaters offering standard motion pictures, there will be multi-screen presentations such as IMAX and motion controlled exhibitions. These presentations will have the audience experiencing a feeling of participation much like the Disney World rides. These presentations will be sponsored by large international corporations to showcase their products.

At home, there will be the home theater. A small television projector, not much larger than today's 13" television receiver, will hang from the rear wall and project a picture whose size is only limited by the size of the room. Or, if you would prefer, a 3" thick, liquid crystal, direct viewing television screen will be mounted on the wall in front of the seating area. This television will also be as large as the room can accommodate. Both of these HDTV (High Definition TV) formats will have dimension ratios of 16 wide by 9 high.

Once again, the picture source can be a video tape, or, more likely, cable or satellite. The movie can even be downloaded from the Internet. Of course, the sound will be played through multiple speakers, in digital stereo. There will be a choice of language, as well as a "second audio program" which offers descriptions of the action for the visually impaired viewers.

Reflections on John F. Vorisek

I sat next to a gentleman at a blackjack table in Atlantic City not long ago. As we talked, I recognized that there was something to this man that showed a world of experience in some specialized area. He didn't seem like a psychologist, or a doctor, or a lawyer. One thing was for sure -- he was a damn good blackjack player. Finally, John Vorisek introduced himself and we began trading professional experiences. John is one half of the legendary Vorisek Brothers, who are famous in the film industry. There work is unseen by the public, because they are behind the scenes, and because they deal with sound. As a team with an international reputation, they worked on movies, mixing together as many as sixty sound tracks into the final sound track that we all hear in the movie theaters. They have done the sound for over a hundred films, including All That Jazz, Arthur, Midnight Cowboy, Serpico, and The Untouchables. Additionally they worked on hundreds of television programs including all of the Honeymooners episodes and over two hundred Walter Cronkite 20th Century programs. With these credentials, the remarks of John Vorisek cannot be taken lightly.

It is interesting to note his comment that in the next few years the multiplex theaters will be replaced by entertainment complexes. One wonders with the tremendous amount of investments necessary to build these extensive and luxurious complexes, how much will a theater ticket cost? In the area of sound, it is amazing to think about having language choices as you watch a film. We've come a long way since the 1920's, when Al Jolson's voice debuted the first "talking" movie.

BARRY FARBER - Radio Broadcaster

Q: What will the future of radio and television look like?

A: First of all, it is already coming into fragmentation. Once upon a time if you entered the business and you were on television, even a local show, everybody in town saw you. Today, you can be on network shows and still be hiding out from the FBI. That type of fragmentation is going to continue. You will notice the evening news is going to be the national bullet where 15 - 20% of the American public depend on it. A lot of the paradigms that they think are shifting are not going to shift. Books on computers are going to start out weak and gradually taper off. People are not going to want to read about yesterday's baseball games from a laptop on a train. The newspapers, the magazines -- these things are going to be embattled as people predict their demise. But those predictions are not coming true.

Q: Why do you think it is not going to happen?

A: Because it is natural and organic to hold a book in your hand, turn pages, put it down -- so there is an awful lot of hype for hype's sake. The same is true for the Internet. I think the Internet is going to disappoint a lot of people. After the initial "Holy Mackerel! I can read a web site in Morocco" and people say "How are you going to keep them down on the farm after they see Paris?" Well, after they check out the Moroccan web sites they are going to stay on the farm. Do you remember the CB radio? Whatever happened to it? I'm not saying the Internet is going to go away -- it will be here and people will use it. But a sophistication is going to set in. Why do I predict this? In the early days of the computer, people overused it. They put recipes on their home computers and made files -- what utter nonsense. They went back to the pen, pencil and pad. So the Internet will be a big disappointment. It will become very fragmented, much like television is. It will go into niche, into niche, into niche. They told a story about a young medical student who was going to be a specialist. His father was an eye, ear, nose and throat specialist. He said dad was too broad -- he wanted to specialize in just the nose. His father said, "Which nostril?" I'll wrap this up with a story. I don't know if you are interested in these anecdotes or not, but the day I destroyed a teaching machine gave me my present mind set. In the early 60's there was a press conference announcing a new teaching machine. What it did was flash text on the screen and the student would master the text and push a button to go on to the next screen -- not the next page mind you -- the next screen of text. I wasn't brilliant enough to sort this out, but I had help. The text was an Army Spanish book that I had read and studied in the Army. So I had the benefit of knowing this magic screen didn't come down from Mt. Olympus -- it was coming out of an old Army book. The presentation talked about the ease of which you could go forward and backward -- and it only cost $18,000. They were nice enough to announce that for school districts, they were happy to talk about financing. When it came time to ask a question I said that $18,000 didn't sound like too much for something that can really teach, but I knew of another product that was flexible enough to allow you to move back and forth through it and is also portable -- it's called a book. I asked what the advantage of the new machine was over a book. I never got a very good answer.

To this day, I am aware of the sheer fun of the computer. But you must realize that the fun wears off. You must recognize the real value of the computer. You have to recognize what lasts and what doesn't. What lasts is the ability to move the cursor up and down, change a word, add a new paragraph, or update something. I am aware of the thrill of flashing lights like a child with a toy -but that is what is going to go away. When people get tired of looking at the 201h Century "hit them in the head" technology -- it will not completely collapse or completely go away, but it will find its place. And its place will not be nearly as exalted as the wise men predict. So wait about 100 years and see whether I am a wise man or a wise guy.

Reflections on Barry Farber

I have known Barry for decades and I consider him one of the most erudite voices in all of broadcasting. He syndicates his talk show throughout the United States. I have appeared countless times on his show, often for hours at a time. I have told him before, that if the bomb somehow dropped, he would instrumental in raising the spirit of society. He can describe a gray rock sitting on a barren road with such dynamic color and fervor that it would spark life into the person listening to his commentary. His conversations are sheer poetry. To develop a true appreciation for the spoken language, listen to Barry talk. He speaks over a dozen languages fluently and a dozen more enough to get by. He has a brilliant ear for the spoken word.

His comments for this book offer me a positive hope that man will not end up sitting with an object in his hand reading screens of text from left to right. Barry puts these devices in its proper place. He says, "people are not going to want to read about yesterday's baseball game from a laptop on a train." I think that says it all. I can't imagine reading such information from a laptop.

ED RHOADES - Authority on the Phantom

As an artist, writer and educator, I see the computer as our most dramatic instrument of change, and it's still in its infancy.

Yet computers just might present us with the millennium's greatest disaster. Experts have forewarned us of the threat of problems posed by Y2K (the year 2000 bug) which among other things, could cause airlines to lose telemetry and banks to lose user account information. The operation of elevators and life saving devices in hospitals could be effected. Even national security may be compromised by inaccessible data locked into older COBAL programs.

However, once these problems are worked out, computers will provide the millennium with subtle and gradual changes that will have far reaching effects. Art forms will rapidly mutate to fit into the new medium of digital information. The number of people reading newspapers online will increase. E-mail, so much faster and more efficient than postal delivery or faxes, will leave only packages and legal documents to be delivered by hand. The printed page will become the exception rather than the rule. The instantaneous exchange of information in education, medicine, business and entertainment has already become the norm. And, the ability to talk with someone while watching him or her on your monitor is already available and improving in quality every day. Like the telephone in the 50's, soon there will be one in every home.

The media will understand that survival necessitates becoming a part of the new order and the computer will replace television as a link to the world.

For a while, new innovations will be entertaining diversions. 3-D holograms, interactive options, sound reproduction, and imagery from high-resolution data will make virtual media seem magical.

But eventually, perfect special effects will be so commonplace that they will no longer be a novelty. When that happens, everyone involved in creative endeavors will be able, once again, to focus on content.

Reflections on Ed Rhoades

Ed Rhoades is a preeminent educator. We came to know each other through our mutual interest in the writings of Lee Falk. Rhoades has become an authority on one of Falk's most popular creations, The Phantom, and has written extensively on the subject in books and magazine articles. Rhoades' knowledge and expertise in the world of cartooning, his work as an educator, and his background as artist and writer give him a unique perspective on the upcoming millennium. Rhoades expresses concern about the millennium's great potential disaster - the computer bug Y2K. This possible crisis has been predicted, analyzed and discussed at great lengths by many over the past year, but Rhoades dramatic reasoning and predicted impacts are interesting.

Equally interesting is Rhoades' prediction that only packages and legal documents will be delivered by the post office in coming years. With computers gaining acceptance and access to them becoming cheaper and more proliferated, E-mail communication will certainly become a standard.

Rhoades' other prediction dealt with special effects in movies and television. Steven Spielberg recently made comments similar to Rhoades'. Spielberg said special effects were being overused in Hollywood and moviemakers would need to return to the story telling format, a la Katherine Hepburn/Spencer Tracy movies, instead of relying on the special effects "crutch." As psychologists and advertisers have known for quite a while, stimuli sustained over a period of time begins to lose its impact. Even a prick on the back of a hand, if continued over time, will stop hurting as the body becomes numb to it. If the special effects in movies become so commonplace, as Rhoades predicts, they will lose their novelty impact. The industry will have to look elsewhere to capture the audience's attention. As Rhoades so eloquently suggests, perhaps the most ideal direction for filmmakers to go is to focus on content. I think this entry will prove to be remarkably accurate.

Phil Thomas - Talk Show Expert

The New Millennium will bring with it many changes in the television industry. Here are a few of my thoughts.

On talk shows: The Talk Show factories will foster a whole new breed of Hosts -- younger, bolder, braver, with boundless energy, annoying personalities and attitudes that directly reflect the culture and time. To see the beginnings of this trend one has to look no further than Rosie O'Donnell, Donny and Marie, Chris Rock, and Jim Henson. One has to wonder who will be next, Bart Simpson? Also, look for talk shows to be called something new, possible "Bitch Sessions!" There will be one rating system in the talk category ... G ... which stands for "Good Luck!"

The reason for the longevity of the talk format is clear -- it is the cheapest form of television production. Many channels, particularly on cable, operate twenty-four hours a day. That causes a huge demand for product to air. With the influx of channels on the cable dial, there isn't enough product to go around. Talk shows, cheaply produced, are the natural time filler. Imagine what the talk show industry will be like in ten years when another hundred channels are added to the cable dial.

In the new millennium the talk show will be more visual than its predecessors of the nineties. Cyberspace, modern technology, and an increase in the cable channel selections will demand that TV producers meet the needs of the young audience. The standard guest segments will be augmented with call-ins, polls, games and lotteries.

On television audiences: Sponsors, always interested in the young buyers, will influence the move to "youth oriented" programming. Advertisers used to purchase time on shows covering an audience age bracket of 18 to 47. Now they want demographics between 12 and 35. These target markets include the last two generations, a viewing audience that has the lowest IQ in history, a seventh grade reading level, and the attention span of an ant. Children don't have to think. They can run to the computer, pull up the Internet, access the subject they are interested in, and have their work done for them.

On technology: Whether it be a mouse or a remote control, a single computer "tooler" will replace everything we now do with our TVs, phones, vcr's, and cd's. The computer will colorize (don't tell Ted Turner) and edit. It will be a complete entertainment center in a small compact size. The "tooler" will become the great instrument of the 21st century -- controlling our lives -- bringing us closer to obesity and stupidity.

On HDTV: High Definition Television (HDTV) will come into play with great passion, but it will not change the industry. It will just make it clearer. Now, that's progress! Forget about medicine and science, we need a clearer picture! First things first.

There will be no more free TV. It will all be Pay TV.

Newton Milnow once said, "Television is a vast wasteland!" Give that man a cigar.

Reflections on Phil Thomas

When it comes to the future of talk shows, there is no better person to reflect on the coming millennium than Phil Thomas. I have known Phil since he worked on *The Mike Douglas Show*. He had his hands in everything on that show, from choreography to pre-interviewing to question preparation. He was a counselor and pacifier to a wide array of people who worked on that program. Phil is also a playwright with a biting sense of humor. Within a few seconds of any conversation with Phil, you are assured of hearing some of the most inane, hilarious and satirically pertinent comments on the passing scene. He is a vibrant character who is truly a hidden gem in the industry.

When I look back on the thousands of celebrities Phil Thomas has worked with over the years, I feel very fortunate to have been able to work with him. Not only did he help coordinate my Mike Douglas appearances, but when I had my television series he worked with me and co-produced many of the dramatic segments. Before television, Phil worked in Las Vegas, handling celebrities and high rollers. When we first met, I asked him why he left his Las Vegas life. His remark was succinct yet completely explained his decision. He simply said to me, "Kreskin -- can you imagine New Year's Eve - 365 days a year?"

A couple of decades back, I remember the signs of the demise of the talk show were evident. *The Mike Douglas Show* ended, as did *The Merv Griffith Show*. There programs had become important parts of our lives, but even with their end, Phil predicted, "The talk show will always be with us. It may alter in its style and form, but it will always be with us. It is one of the cheapest shows to create in all of broadcasting." I foresee talk shows in the future being designed for special audiences. As television channel choices proliferate, some talk shows will aim at a younger market, and others will aim at the increasingly important senior citizen market.

Within the next decade, the senior market may become the biggest market of all.

Currently, certain talk shows are exploiting sensationalism. The Jerry Springer boxing matches are a prime example. This show is at the very least unconsciously choreographed. The participants have all seen the show and know what is expected of them. The violence becomes shock with a major impact on the viewers. There is a very real downside to this sensational talk format -- the longevity is remarkably limited.

I remember a few years ago when Bill Boggs was co-producing a show out of WOR in New Jersey called The *Morton* Downey *Show.* The program was Jerry Springer's precursor. There was shouting, confrontations, and arguments that were incredibly intense. Before my appearance on the show, I sat in the control room will Phil, a feeling of queasiness building in my stomach. Phil asked me, "How much longer, Kreskin?" I said to him, "Three more months." The show went off the air two months and three weeks later.

While appearing on The *Morton Downey Show* was against my better judgement, it was a worthwhile experience. Downey had been a fan of mine for years, and had seen me frequently in Las Vegas. He always treated me with the kind of care and respect I would afford him, or any professional. So, when he asked me to do the show, I agreed. The show itself taught me something about human nature. I remember vividly the setting. I was up on stage, and the audience was cast as antagonists. I was interrupted by a female in the audience who fired a victoryolic jab towards me. However, when the show went to commercial, she came up to me and told me that she was a tremendous fan of mine. Her contrasting behavior demonstrated "stage hypnosis." People on stage take on behavior patterns that are expected of them. When she confronted me on the air, she was role playing, much like an actress would. The lesson is clear. No longer can people appear on talk shows as innocent everyday citizens -- they have already been contaminated by watching the shows over and over and seeing the behavior that is expected of them.

Recently, during a two show appearance with Howie Mandel, I was in my dressing room between tapings. I heard a knock on my dressing room door, and was pleased upon opening it to see an old friend, Fred DeCordova. I had the pleasure of working with Fred during his years as the director of *The Tonight Show with Johnny Carson.* However, Fred also directed the Jack Benny program, as well as other legendary productions. Fred's incredible accomplishments in the broadcast industry leave him with few peers of his stature. We reflected for twenty minutes or so on the passing show business scene. We discussed how many of the talents of the past had a certain quality that is just not found in today's crop of performers. Many of today's stars rely on schtick and shock, as opposed to talent.

SKITCH HENDERSON - Musical Conductor

I interviewed Skitch Henderson to glean his predictions for the new millennium.

Q: The symphonic scene is drastically changing, isn't it Skitch?

A: It certainly is.

Q: Tell me a little about it.

A: The most dramatic change is the financial side. The current environment makes situations like my Pop's Symphony at Carnegie Hall almost unaffordable. It is hard to resolve the financial problem because of the high cost of living in today's society. The thing that saves me at Carnegie Hall, and you would understand this, is that I only have to hire my orchestra for the season. In years past, the normal situation would have me owning the orchestra outright. My costs would include their entire livelihood. As it is now, my strings play mostly Mozart, the woodwinds are the alternate theme at the Metropolitan Opera, the brass players are an assortment of gypsies, and the percussion players include, as we say, "short hairs." Those are temporary players who I can pay less. I have been forced into this situation. If I had to own the orchestra outright I wouldn't be in business.

Q: So your orchestra does other work as well?

A: We lay out everything about a year or so in advance. Right now, we have scheduled through 2001. Because of the current financial situation, you must be very organized to make sure you have enough funds to keep it all going?

Q: Skitch, what do you think is going to happen in the next century with electronics playing a larger part in music?

A: Well, I've never been a big supporter of electronics. However I have to confess that I am probably wrong. Conductors like Michael Gillson Thomas in San Francisco have been on the forefront experimenting with what you and I would call contemporary sounds. He has been working on incorporating those sounds into the symphonic world. I think it's a bear that is going to go over the mountain if we don't adapt in some way to what is happening. I don't think you are going to hear Beethoven and Mozart, Brookner and Brahms. While the trend includes this type of music, I don't think the repertoire that has been written for symphonic orchestras in the last 30 or 40 years will bear longevity.

Q: Do you think orchestras will remain as large? Will there always have to be large orchestras in some areas?

A: There would have to be because of the repertoire. I don't think that will change. Remember the word "ego." Some of it is ego of sound and not necessarily ego of personality. It is the individual ego of the sound structure.

Q: You mentioned on the wonderful PBS 80th Birthday Part at Carnegie Hall that in the early days of jazz there was much improvisation in music and that the improvisation had since disappeared. Do you think improvisation will return?

A: I personally think it is very healthy. Many scholars are violently opposed to it. I think improvisation might be the salvation of this whole structure that we live in. There are young soloists who now have improvised in the repertoire and made it successful. I think there will have to be changes.

Q: With the proliferation of cable and the endless stations in television, do you think music is going to become more and more compartmentalized, as I suspect is going to happen with much of the other fair in entertainment and broadcasting?

A: I think it will be totally categorized. When I book artists for Carnegie, especially when we book based on themes, we cater to the differences in our audiences. In the upcoming season, I am going to do something I thought I would never do in my life. I am going to do a Hawaiian show in Hawaii. It takes me back to when I was a kid, it was wonderful to hear the radio broadcasts from Hawaii.

Q: The only time I heard Hawaiian music regularly when I was a kid was when Haliloke sang it on the Arthur Godfrey Show.

A: Everybody was so excited when I suggested it because we haven't done that for so long.

Q: I have heard very little Hawaiian music in recent years. For a while country music was dominating the scene, but something seems to have even happened in that area as well. I have done a lot with the Nashville Network (TNN), but recently I see the talent pool less qualified. I even see soap stars singing country music. The music seems to have become so diluted that it has lost something. After all, I think of the heritage of the true country music star. Do you see the same trends?

A: Well, it has become so contemporary. Do you remember when it was Country Western? I guess we called them country singers -- shades of Eddie Arnold.

Q: I know Eddie Arnold and I know Crystal Gayle. Something has been lost in the scene. I don't want to mention who, but a national figure confided to me during a commercial break on a TNN show that if you listen to a certain person (and he meant a very famous country singer) his music has gotten too loud. Skitch, I have a very high sense of hearing, yet I find when it gets too loud I don't seem to hear it anymore. Does that make sense?

A: Absolutely! I still love the acoustical sound. I have worked through the years with Chet Atkins and we have discussed this.

Q: On a personal note, when you presented your 80th Birthday Concert at Carnegie Hall, you ended with the song "Till We Meet Again." I heard that song more than any other in my household, as it was my mother's favorite and she would sing it often. She is approaching 94 years of age and she still sings it. It must be special for you as well.

A: I have always had a special thing about that song. Every once in a while, if I have a singer that I absolutely trust, I will do that song as an encore at symphonic concerts.

Reflections on Skitch Henderson

Skitch and I go back to the 1960's when television was live. Skitch was the musical conductor and arranger on many television shows, including *The Tonight Show with Steve Allen*. When Johnny Carson took over the Tonight Show, Skitch was his musical conductor for a number of years, as well as the pianist. Skitch then went on to host his own daily television talk program out of New York. Skitch worked for many years in the film industry as a pianist and arranger.

I worked with Skitch on a number of television programs, including my own. He appeared on my pilot and when the show went into general production, I flew him up to Canada where we filmed my show. He appeared on two of my programs. For one particularly memorable segment I asked him to tape a simple song of his choosing and make certain that no one would know what song was on the tape. Before he came up to Canada, he sent his secretary and all personnel out of his studio and sat at the piano alone. He recorded a short, simple song. He brought the recording up to the taping in Canada. Once we went on the air live, I picked a stranger from the audience. Neither Skitch nor I had ever met or talked with this woman before. I had her stand in the audience as I stood in front of her. I recited the standard notes in the singing range - do, re, me, fa, so, la, ti, do. She picked certain notes as they came to her. She recited about a dozen notes. I asked Skitch to play those notes on the piano and the audience smiled when they recognized the children's song Frarajaqua. Skitch had a beaming, bright expression on his face as he played the notes that our audience member seemed to perceive mentally. Skitch then pulled out the tape he made back in the United States and played it on a cassette recorder. The audience erupted in applause when the tape also played Frarajaqua. It was an extremely dramatic segment and one of the highlights of my five and a half years on television. Skitch's contribution of his enthusiasm and sincerity were very important to me.

Years after the Frarajaqua segment with Skitch, I was in a fine restaurant sitting down to a nice meal with Bob Collins, the Publisher and President of Gannett Publishing. I noticed Skitch across the room. We all joined together for dinner and enjoyed a varied and vibrant conversation. Something came up about my ability to play piano. Until that moment, Skitch hadn't known I could play. We decided that I would appear with the New York Pops Orchestra in a concert around Halloween. The program had a Halloween theme and I prepared a rather dramatic test involving the entire orchestra. During my hour of the program, it was decided that I would introduce a song that I had written when I was a child of about thirteen. A few weeks before the performance, I gave Skitch a copy of my song. On the day of the show, I was called from my dressing room at Carnegie Hall in the late afternoon. The assistant said I was wanted in the hall of the theater. When I arrived, Skitch greeted me. He was in shirtsleeves and had been obviously rehearsing. He asked me to take a seat in the audience. While I had attended many functions at Carnegie Hall, this was the first time I sat down for an afternoon performance, and the first time I was the only audience member. Skitch tapped his baton and started conducting the orchestra. I heard, for the first time, my piece played by a symphony. When the piece ended, I rose from my chair with tears in my eyes. I walked onto the stage and thanked Skitch. He pointed to the manuscript on the podium and said, "All of the arrangements are for you to take and use as you wish." I found out later that Skitch had gone away for the weekend to a place where he could work in peace. He spent most of the weekend arranging my song for a full orchestra. I have used this piece often in my concerts with orchestras. It was an incredible gift, and demonstrates the dimension of this man.

It's important to realize that what goes around comes around. How we treat and relate to those in our lives can reflect in the way others treat us. This is true in the memories of what is given and taken in life.

ED McMAHON

I think the biggest change from the standpoint of television and the viewer will be the one that gives the viewer incredible control over what they watch. As television gets more and more intertwined with the computer, the viewer will be able to actually control the television screen.

Imagine a political poll that is instantaneous and country wide.

Imagine a drama that has three possible endings and the audience selects the one they want to watch.

Imagine that in an instant one can learn the "mood" of the country. What's "hot" and what's not!

Television schedules will go out the windows. If you want to see NYPD Blue at breakfast, it's yours "on demand."

And television will be everywhere. It will be in your car, on every street corner, in the sky on cloud formations, and on your wrist.

Finally, the viewer will determine who wins the title of Miss America - in an instant!

Reflections on Ed McMahon

I have known Ed McMahon for over 30 years. What more can I say that hasn't already been said about him. He is truly a giant in the broadcasting industry. He went from selling juice on the Atlantic City boardwalk to playing a clown on a local television show to broadcasting immortality. My introduction to him was much the same way as the rest of the world's - seeing him as the co-anchor with Johnny Carson. I first met him in person when I appeared on the Carson Show when it was being broadcast from New York. At the time, Carson liked to book guests in two's, so I appeared on the show with my mother. She was not an experienced performer and never envisioned becoming so. As a result, she was very nervous. I remember the kindness and gentleness with which McMahon reassured my mother before she made her television debut before a national audience.

As part of the team that owned the Tonight Show for so many years, one could easily say that Johnny Carson and Ed McMahon were one of the longest running comedy teams in history, along with Abbot & Costello and Laurel & Hardy. McMahon possessed a unique gift for the program. He was so intrinsically tuned in to the host - he knew Carson's whims and he knew his moods and, more importantly, he knew when Carson needed him. I think that is the essential skill of the perfect co-host - knowing when the host needs you and when to stay back. The Tonight Show wasn't quite the same on the nights McMahon was missing just as it wasn't the same on the nights Carson took off. The chemistry between the two and McMahon's inevitable laugh off camera were part of the charm and mystic of the show.

I appeared on the Carson show dozens of times and McMahon was always sitting just to my right. If I needed some assistance with my performance he was already ready. He wouldn't interrupt with remarks or grab at cards. He would always know when a gesture was needed, or a nod of agreement. He has a warm, almost paternal, quality about him. His skills are evident in making his television show Star Search a hit. Arthur Godfrey had been successful with the format for over ten years, but many failed at recreating the concept until McMahon succeeded.

Today's television talk shows are missing those qualities. The chemistry that McMahon and Carson had could also be found between Jack Paar and Hugh Downs, Steve Allen and Skitch Henderson, Merv Griffin and Arthur Treacher. Those pairings made the shows successful.

As for McMahon's predictions, his look at the future of television is startling and some of the most refreshing comments in this book. It's almost scary to think of the potential of instant polling. Additionally, it's very interesting to think about the possibility of the viewership choosing Miss America. I think that many reviewers and journalists will find themselves quoting Ed McMahon's remarks for some time to come. While he has long been considered one of the great straightmen in history, he may have usurped my abilities and turned out to be an incredible prophet.

TERRIE WILLIAMS - Public Relations & Communications Expert

The next millennium will hold new challenges for the public relations industry. There is, and will continue to be, a plethora of information at our fingertips. As the information revolution continues, public relations practitioners will have to find new ways of putting a "personal touch" on their work. Voice mail, faxes and the Internet have all made communication a little less personal. As an industry, we will have to work harder to get back to the basics of our profession. Hand-written notes, face-to-face interaction, and promptly returning phone calls have to become the norm again. Public relations must work to maintain personal relations.

Reflections on Terrie Williams

I have known Terrie Williams for a number of years. She runs a close-knit talent agency in New York City that represents many outstanding people in the entertainment, literary and business worlds. She is a fascinating individual who, in addition to running the talent agency, gives seminars on communications. Years ago I found myself at one of her educational seminars and I was impressed at how easily she is able to touch those with whom she communicates.

Her remarks for this book reflect a concern many contributors have voiced -- the exposure to immense volumes of information. However, she was able to spotlight the issue, pointing out the importance of a solution! While many contributors were able to identify the potential issue, Williams pointed out the need to make a conscious effort to bring back the "personal touch" in business relationships. When unlimited information is available at the snap of our fingers, will we be lost in an endless stream of faxes, voice mail, and computer communications? Williams sees the very real need to look beyond the information and get back to the basics, including face to face communication. I love her comment that phone calls will again need to be promptly returned. For years now, it is a common remark by East Coast entertainers that if you call a talent agency on the West Coast it will takes weeks to get your call returned. This is not merely my expression of dissatisfaction, but the experience of many people with whom I have spoken. And, it is not the blame of the West Coast agencies, it is a sign of the times -- the current "normal" way of doing business. Williams addresses this reality by stating that we must embrace the true meaning of public relations.

Incidentally, as I am writing this entry, I have in front of me a book Williams sent to me. It is a small book, comprising a mere 40 pages. On each page there are only a couple of sentences. The title of the book makes me pick it up from time to time and reflect on a page or two. The book is called "God Made Easy." That sums up the tastes and reflections of Terrie Williams.

PAUL BAKER - Public Relations

The public relations field has gone through innumerable changes in the past fifteen years with the advent of the fax machine, personal computer, videoconference equipment, and the like. All these technological advances have made the delivery of information instantaneous and global with the touch of a button.

Looking forward to the next millennium, I believe technology will continue to march forward with new inventions and new modes of communication, which will again speed the delivery and distribution of information. The universe will become much smaller and easier to access.

The quality of art will certainly increase via downloading off the web, and as a result, technology will facilitate more instantaneous visual applications of the desired message. Furthermore, with video conference capabilities increasing both in quality and availability, more parties will be brought together allowing the sharing of information without the necessity for domestic or international travel.

Clearly, if we all had the mental powers that Kreskin employs, many of these technological wonders would cease to be important.

Reflections on Paul Baker

I have known the public relations firm of Baker, Winokur and Ryder for almost two decades. The two founders, Paul Baker and Larry Winokur, are remarkable success stories. They started out as attorneys, but quickly turned to public relations. Their public relations firm began in a small room in Los Angeles. They had rented a table and two chairs and had two phones installed. The two shared the table as they tried to grow their business. Baker has recounted to me days that were so slow, he would call Winokur on the phone, even though he was sitting three feet away -- at the other end of the rented table! Today, their organization is legendary in show business and one of the largest public relations firms in the world.

In a field that alters human personality and creates larger than life images, I have found Paul Baker to be a person of unique integrity. He has seen it all in the world of show business and has weathered the storm of controversy surrounding clients, all the while maintaining his morals and bearings. Baker gained his interest in show business from his youth. He grew up in Australia, the son of an Australian television star. Because of his father's status, all the prominent Hollywood stars and music personalities that toured or visited Australia would end up in his home for a visit. Baker was fascinated by life and when he was old enough, he left home, travelling into far off lands to seek his own answers to life's questions. His travels took him to Tibet, where he fled just ahead of the Communist invasion, to India, and to other remote locals. He eventually settled in the United States, began his legal training, and eventually started his company.

I recall in discussing this book with him, he wondered whether the merger mania found in many industries, such as banking, would strike the public relations field. He went further to suggest the possibility that there would only be three or four public relation firms of any note left in the United States after a shakeout. I fear that this might come to pass. When industries compact into large unwielding powerhouses, individuality and creativity are left behind. If this were to happen in special professions, such as public relations, the results could only be negative. Public relations thrives on creativity. While trying to spotlight, glamorize and popularize a product or personality, creativity is the one tool that works toward success. Large, sterile, corporate culture does nothing to create an atmosphere where public relation professionals can do their best.

Baker also mentions that instantaneous communication will continue to take place and the increase of video conferencing will eliminate the need for some business travel. This comment has far reaching implications, much past the world of public relations. It is possible that in many fields, travel that in years past was considered a necessity, will become passe. Businesses will cut expenses by facilitating their personnel to travel within the room he sits, via video conferencing. This technology was helpful to me earlier this year. I did two days of promotion for media outlets around the world. I was able to do all of the promotion without traveling. I was set up in a room with a television set, a cameraman, and a sound man. The interviewers were geographically separated from me at distances up to thousands of miles. Only a few years ago, I would have had to travel extensively by plane to effect that much exposure. I wonder if the airlines have reflected on this possible trend from a practical and economic point of view.

MARILYN MICHAELS - Comedian & Impersonator

Comedy, like everything else, is cyclic. Jim Carrey is really the 90's version of Jerry Lewis. At least he sprang from the Jerry Lewis "tree" of broad comedy. So, things repeat themselves. However, today there are more and more women in comedy. It is no longer unfeminine to be funny. There are more funny gals than ever before. What was once the domain of a few courageous females like Phyllis Diller, Joan Rivers, Lucille Ball, and Carol Burnett has changed and now we have a plethora of funny females. So, we are sure to see more of this in the millennium and that's great for Mai!!

Reflections on Marilyn Michaels

Marilyn Michaels and I go back to the days when Johnny Carson's show originated from New York. From the first time I worked with her through the years of watching her on television, I have always thought of her not just as a brilliant comedienne, but as a remarkable impersonator. You can close your eyes and actually envision the people that she is impersonating. She is incredibly accurate.

A personal incident involving Marilyn has become one of the most dramatic events in my life. Marilyn and I were guests on one of Carson's shows. I attempted to demonstrate an experiment that has its origins in the times of ancient spirit mediums. I was using this old technique and extending it with my abilities as a thought-reader. I wanted to not only perceive her thoughts, but to cause her thoughts to manifest themselves in some way. I took a couple of chalkboards and had everyone on the show, including Marilyn, inspect them. They were completely wiped clean. I asked Marilyn to hold the boards together, facing each other. I then took a piece of chalk that I soaked in water, so that it would cling to the chalkboard, and dropped it between the two boards. Finally, it was time to start the trick. I asked Marilyn to think of someone whom she knew early in her life. She reflected pensively and then told me she had someone in mind. I began to reflect and within a minute's time, I had gotten the mental image of the letter "M". I revealed the letter to Marilyn who looked surprised. When I told her the second letter was "0" she began to visible shake. By the time I told her the name was "MOISA" it was clear to the studio audience and those at home that I was accurate, as Marilyn's reaction was so obvious. I then asked her to pull the two chalkboards apart. The wet chalk I had dropped between the two boards, had written out the same name. Marilyn was in shock, and the studio audience erupted into applause as we went to a commercial break. She recounted in a later interview that the person she was thinking of was a Rabbi she remembered from her childhood. She insisted that no one could possibly have known that she would choose that person, since she hadn't thought of the Rabbi in years. It was truly a very successful reading.

Marilyn reflects a great tradition of the female comedy star. She is accurate when she says that the road to success is easier for female comics now, as opposed to years past when only a handful of female comics were successful. She has my admiration and my thanks, for the memory of a rather dramatic moment in my television career.

ARTIE SHAW -jazz great

On my request for predictions for the millennium, Artie wrote: You're the Amazing Kreskin -- so you tell me!

Reflections on Artie Shaw

Artie Shaw is one of the great jazz musicians in modern history. He is also a successful author. I just had to enclose his remarks to demonstrate what a great sense of humor he has. Because of his talent, charm and warmth, Jazz is lucky to have him as a spokesman.

MILT SUCHIN - personal management

The personal management business, which has always stressed "personal" attention and creativity, will no longer exist as we know it today. There will be a continual erosion of the major agency ranks as more and more talent agents defect to the personal management occupation. Managers will begin to wear and inherit many hats that they have not worn before.

As the talent agencies have reinvented themselves from only representing talent to the representation of "packages" (combining all the elements of a project), clothing designers, cartoon characters and even cities, the fine line between managers, personal managers and talent agents has blurred. These areas of representation have encroached upon each other's territories for years, but as the cost of doing business in the entertainment industry rises, some of these representation functions will evaporate and the relationships will become acrimonious.

One of the main reasons that prevent personal managers from pursuing more of the agent's functions is the prohibition and strict regulation of the agent profession. In most major cities, it is a violation of law for a manager to solicit or negotiate employment. Talent agents are licensed and regulated under the employment laws. The newly ordained managers will picket for legislative changes allowing them more freedom.

As more talent agents change occupations there will be the birth of a specialization credit occurring whereupon those talent representatives will carve out a niche in specific fields.

The bottom line -- only the aggressive, bright and knowledgeable will achieve that benchmark referred to as success.

Reflections on Milt Suchin

I value Milt Suchin's speculations on the coming millennium, having known him for almost two decades. Not only has he personally managed me for a number of years, but he has acted as a trusted counsel and sounding board for many of the career decisions I have made in recent years. Milt's longest and most established client is Phyllis Diller. His reputation for incredible loyalty to his clients is legendary. Today I consider him a personal friend.

Milt has a fascinating background. He started out studying law, and then found his way into one of the major booking agencies in New York. As part of his job, he would visit New York's nightclubs every day, taking in the regular shows that start around 8:00 PM and then the late shows that run into the wee hours of the morning. Working as an agent gave him the experience and familiarity with the workings of the agencies. When he moved into the personal management field, his background as an agent helped him communicate and deal with agents much more effectively.

Milt would be the first to agree that for some diabolical reason agents in show business have a horrible reputation. The negative reputation isn't always earned, but it does seem to be a tradition. I remember a quote Merv Griffin passed on to me from Fred Allen. Allen was a pioneer radio humorist, who was renowned for his generosity. He would often leave his studio in New York after a radio broadcast and be seen handing out money to performers who had seen their time in the limelight pass. With that sympathy for the performer in mind, Allen once said, "You could put all the sincerity in Hollywood in the navel of a flea with room to spare for four sesame seeds and the heart of an agent!"

As for Suchin's comments, his remark that the personal management business will no longer exist as we know it today is quite interesting. He mentions the erosion of major agency ranks as agents defect into personal management occupations. One wonders if there is a hidden message amongst his reflections that one or two large and powerful agencies will exist as an umbrella over all the actions of everyone in show business. This trend certainly seems to be happening in the banking industry, and it seems to be happening in other markets, such as movie theaters and department stores. The question is whether the individual will survive, or is the handwriting already on the wall, as we see mom and pop stores disappearing from the United States. Years ago, the legendary nighttime radio broadcaster Barry Gray once said to me how he noticed so many actors leaving one of the major agencies in New York because they waned more personal attention and felt they were becoming lost in the shuffle. I wonder if more and more professional people involved in all kinds of specialized jobs find themselves lost in the shuffle.

CHRIS BROWNE - cartoonist (Hagar the Horrible)

In Hagar's day, illuminated books were the property of only the wealthy. The only way a working stiff like Hagar could lay his hands on some night table reading was to swipe it! Now, a thousand years later, anyone can get their hands on a book or a newspaper. There is, however, a new elite -- those with a personal computer.

Computers are changing every facet of life, and cartooning is no exception. These days you can typically find a cartoonist's e-mail address right on the cartoon. Boom -- you're in touch -- direct! Beyond this, some cartoonists have gone so far as to invite the public to contribute gags to their features. And, some syndicate web sites feature interactive cartoon environments and games.

One cartoonist I know, Brooke McEldowney, draws his wonderful comic strip, Nine Chickweed Lane, ENTIRELY on a MacIntosh computer with a Wacom drawing tablet. He draws the cartoon with a plastic pen that contains no ink or lead -- the drawing appears on his computer screen! Brooke's studio is completely free of paper clutter. One of the hidden benefits to working this way is that fewer trees are used up.

It is not hard to imagine complete interactive cartoon worlds where you could be completely immersed in the cartoonist's vision. All you need is memory and bandwidth -- and experts are working on those problems right now!

What is likely is that Americans will be seeing much more cheaply produced, mass marketed, overly violent and overly sexual material creeping into the marketplace. This has been a direction for years, and the dam break is due at almost any moment. I LOVE comics, but I am not looking forward to this. However, that is only one direction comics will take. Some comics will take the other, higher road. They will be smart, witty, and heartfelt works. We've already seen some of these remarkable strips in the past few years. For Better Or For Worse, Calvin and Hobbes, Cathy, and Doonesbury have shown the way.

Reflections on Chris Browne

Chris Browne is the son of the award-winning cartoonist Dick Browne. He assisted his father on the comic strips "Hi and Lois" and "Hagar the Horrible." Since his father's passing in 1989, Chris has continued to write and draw "Hagar the Horrible" which now appears in almost 2,000 newspapers around the world, translated into 13 languages in 58 countries.

Chris Browne seems to reflect what we have seen in some of the commentary in this book, including Roger Ebert's remarks on movies. They see trends in the communication areas where the viewer will become more interactive with the medium. With violence in our television programming, in movies, and even on radio, Browne's prediction that cartoons will also trend towards sex and violence seems accurate. One wonders how the prediction of more interaction will effect the prediction of stronger violence and sexuality in communication.

Politics, Law & Crime

KENNETH STARR -- Independent Counsel

In September of 1998, Kenneth Starr forwarded to Congress a 445 page report outlining what he considered to be substantial and credible evidence that the President of the United States had committed impeachable offenses. The result was a firestorm of political activity. Kenneth Starr was appointed by Attorney General, and Clinton appointee, Janet Reno, as an independent investigator to look into alleged misdeeds by the President. The September report represented his findings on certain areas of his investigations. Starr had been a judge and was a top lawyer when appointed by Reno to investigate the President. He is certainly in tune with Constitutional law and counts a number of the Supreme Court Justices as friends. We met with him in June of 1998, in Washington DC.

Q: Do you see any major changes in law coming up?

A: That's an interesting question. I think American law is fairly rooted in precedent.

Q: What about things like tort reform?

A: Those types of issues are handled by the legislature. The courts tend to create trends by either being liberal or conservative, and that is usually based on Presidential appointment opportunities.

Q: Do you think Congress might pass some type of tort reform?

A: The lobbies are very powerful. I think some type of legislation will eventually pass. The extent and implications are hard to foresee.

Q: Do you think the court will become more conservative or more liberal?

A: This court? (asking about the Supreme Court)

Q: OK.

A: The Justices make up their own mind on issues. Presidents have avoided creating specific litmus tests. But on the whole, I would expect the court to become more conservative. There will probably be no more appointments during the current administration, and I would think the next President will be Republican.

Starr predicts there will be some type of Tort reform legislation passed but is not sure of how far reaching it might be. He also predicts that the first President of the next millennium will be Republican and the next Supreme Court appointee will be conservative.

Reflections on Kenneth Starr

We should understand that Kenneth Starr was asked these questions in June of 1998. Since that time, the President was impeached by the House of Representatives and voted not to be removed by the Senate. Kenneth Starr came under attack for his zeal and perceived obsession with "getting the president." This type of characterization is common in nearly all criminal prosecutions. It is an effort to deflect the guilt of the accused by turning the focus on the methods of the police of the prosecutor. However, many defenders of the President feel Starr went too far.

I do find it significant that he predicts the next president will be Republican.

CLARENCE THOMAS -- Supreme Court Justice

The President of the United States is usually regarded as the most powerful man in the world. However, an argument can be made that the nine men and woman sitting on the Supreme Court of the United States have a greater impact and wield greater power. The Supreme Court Justices are life-long appointees and they have the power to strike down laws and treaties passed by Congress and the President. Clarence Thomas is one of these nine justices. His power and influence on the United States is immense.

Q: Do you think the court will address any huge landmark issues in the coming years?

A: We spend a good deal of time choosing cases. They all have importance.

Q: I'm talking about cases like abortion, that would capture the attention of the country.

A: I really couldn't tell you. The cases are reviewed as they come to us.

Q: But if the court wanted to overturn legalized abortion, you could cherry-pick a case to base the decision on.

A: We can certainly pick our cases, but I know of no pressing need to address the abortion issue.

Q: How about any other mainstream legal issue?

A: The most widely reported cases coming up are the ones testing the President's executive privileges.

Q: I'm looking more into the future. Any legal trends or possible big cases.

A: Like I said, all of our cases hold importance. I cannot tell you what we might do next term.

Clarence Thomas held his, and the court's, future plans tight to the vest. He clearly did not want to give any indication of where the court might be headed. But he did seem to predict that the abortion issue will not be addressed by this court any time soon. This would mean that for the foreseeable future, there will be no change to legalized abortion.

Reflections on Clarence Thomas

There has probably been no Supreme Court Justice who has gotten more publicity than Clarence Thomas. He seems very comfortable in making appearances and commentaries at banquets and other events. The Supreme Court Justices are a group of powerful figures that traditionally remain hidden from the public eye. However, Thomas is truly a talented public communicator and flexes his skill at many events.

It is interesting that this entry follows Kenneth Starr, as it makes me wonder what the Senate Hearings for Thomas' confirmation would have been like if Clarence Thomas had an independent counsel appointed to investigate the Anita Hill situation. In those days, the hearings were much dirtier and full of mud slinging and I wonder how long they would have lasted with a independent counsel investigation attached. I thank God that it never came to that as we have a brilliant and highly respected man on the court in Clarence Thomas.

DAVID BERKOWITZ - The Son of Sam

David Berkowitz #78A1 976
Sullivan Correctional Facility
P.O. Box AG
Fallsburg, NY 12733-0116

Dear Mr. Kreskin:

Thank you for your letter of June 9th. I am sorry to take so long to get back to you, but I misplaced your letter in a box with some other papers. If I am too late for your publication, I am sorry. But I hope you will be interested in what I have to share.

By the way, I do not know what your first name is, so I simply wrote "Alan." Prison rules require correspondence that is outgoing to have a full first and last name. They would be suspicious if I wrote "Amazing."

Over the years many things have transpired in my life. There was a time, as you know, when I was an evil and ugly person. However, about eleven years ago I had a very moving spiritual experience. In Christian terminology we call it being "born again."

Anyhow, although many may scoff, the experience was very real and I believe with all my heart that God has done something wonderful in my life. Having a spiritual experience will certainly not change my circumstances. I still have consecutive life sentences to do totaling (sic) more than 300 years.

However, today I do have peace. I also know that I have God's forgiveness even though society will probably never forgive me. I have to live with this, and I feel Christ has given me the strength and the hope. I will enclose a few testimonial pamphlets that may help to make clear the things that are happening today in my life. More than twenty years ago the devil made me into a murderer. Today Jesus Christ has made me into a minister.

Thank you for the opportunity to share what I see for the future concerning prison and other things. Yours truly,

David Berkowitz

encl
cc

TO: The Amazing Kreskin
FR: David Berkowitz   September 10, 1998

I see prisons in America as becoming increasingly violent and hopeless places. Prisons have become the burial grounds of society's unwanteds. As people become increasingly intolerant of criminal activity, and as the Nation becomes more like a "Police State" with each passing day, our prisons will continue to fill up with young men, mostly the urban poor.

I have seen so many cutbacks and closings of rehabilitative programs. This will continue. Punishment and not rehabilitation will become the order of the day.

As America's economy weakens and as the pressures of life for its citizens increase, America's prison population will continue to rise. More prisons are going to be built and "Corrections" will continue to be a booming industry.

I believe that one day America's economy will fail and we will enter an age of tremendous hardship. Martial law will be declared as America's cities become war zones and as the populace is thrown into a panic. Thus, for those who are already incarcerated when these things come to pass, life in America's prisons will become a living hell. I feel that we are headed for anarchy and extreme social upheaval.

I also believe that, one day in the future, America's prisons are going to be instantaneously - within the space of about one day's time - be turned into places of confusion when it turns out that tens of thousands of inmates from all levels of security classifications suddenly disappear into thin air.

Now you're probably saying to yourself, "This man is crazy! Is Berkowitz living in a fantasy world?" No! Let me explain why I believe this...

You see, even though we often think of prisons as places of darkness and despair, there has been a ray of hope behind these walls. Over the years many ministers have come into prisons to preach the gospel. These ministers caused many inmates to take a look at their own lives, and what they saw they did not like. I myself took a look inside of myself. I realized after someone shared the gospel with me that I needed to repent and to ask God's forgiveness.

Although much of the general public would mock this, many prisoners have given their lives to God. They have changed for the better with God's help. This, unfortunately, is the one side of prison the public doesn't (sic) get to see. But it is good and many of these men are sincere.

It is Christ's plan to instantly remove His people from earth to heaven. Because many prisoners are now Christians, they too (and myself) will be included in this miraculous event. However, the disappearance of millions of people around the world as well as tens of thousands of prison inmates will cause chaos and confusion everywhere.

I do not know when these things will happen, but it may be soon. Thank you for allowing (sic) to share. I know that I have written far too much for you to use. But I believe you will find all this very interesting.

God bless you, Mr. Kreskin.

Reflections on David Berkowitz

I had some mixed feelings about requesting the reflections of this monstrous killer, but I had a larger purpose in mind. Throughout my life, I have had relatives involved in law enforcement. This closeness to the field has given me insight into the challenges of the job. I see the work of a policeman today to be infinitely more difficult than in a bygone era. Respect for authority is diminishing almost daily, while at the same time, a policeman is forced to be a crime fighter, attorney, psychologist, sociologist, and parent. The skill and effort required to be an effective police officer is immense. It is embarrassing to note the low salaries of some of the most important people in our society - policemen and teachers. If our societal priorities were in sync, policemen and teachers would be among the highest paid professionals. The tragedy of police work today is that the public appreciates them only after we need them.

With these thoughts on crime fighting in mind, I requested the reflections of David Berkowitz. The tragedy, violence and evil he inflicted on the lives of so many people gives me very strong mixed emotions about his very survival. How many criminals suddenly discover God, only after they are in prison? If their beliefs are as sincere as they expound, they certainly wouldn't fight the death penalty. The opportunity to be put to death should be a welcome salvation for them.

While I consider myself a religious person with very deep convictions, I have become increasingly suspicious of this endless array of people who discover God after they are hopelessly incarcerated. The statistics illustrate that many of them are released on parole and then repeat their heinous crimes. I have become increasingly convinced that in the case of violent crimes, the '.parole key" should simply be thrown away.

Years ago, early in my career, I shared an office with a Clinical Psychologist by the name of Dr. Harold Hansen. Dr. Hansen provided me with an education that I could have never received in any college. Despite my rigorous studies and a degree in Psychology being awarded to me from Seton Hall University, I credit Dr. Hansen with some of my most important training. He believed in my ability to help others. We would discuss everything, from sociology to psychologists to those who ran penal institutions. Dr. Hansen concluded through these discussions that there is a small percentage of criminals who simply cannot be rehabilitated. Various new age, modern psychoanalytic and psychotherapeutic thought has made this concept very unpopular through the years. However, it is a conclusion that Dr. Hansen believed in throughout his life. If this conclusion is true, then there is a criminal element with which we must deal on a permanent basis. If the death penalty is too unappealing to society, or too impractical in our court system, a large institution should be built in some remote area, perhaps the Grand Canyon, where these criminals can be incarcerated permanently.

I have decided that Berkowitz would be the only criminal mind, outside of politics, that I would grapple with in this book. For God's sake, let's throw the keys away!

MARVIN FISH - Attorney

In the next millennium, the role of the attorney will be multi-dimensional. With taxes, profit motive and cost containment being so important, they will impact most issues presented to lawyers. Basic familiarity with those factors will no longer be sufficient. The public is concerned with duration, prolongation, and quality of life, as well as the time and circumstances of its termination. Those values will have an impact on personal injury claims, insurance claims, health care planning, living wills, estate planning, governmental subsidies and the right of autonomy to be applied to the enjoyment of one's life and assets. Medical knowledge by attorneys will be essential. Continually growing concern for values such as truth, honesty, autonomy, integrity, faithfulness, reliability, accountability, morality and religiosity needs to be reflected in personal relationships such as trustees, partners, employees, proxies and prospective spouses. Attorneys need to have more than just a working knowledge of psychology and ethics. Even if the attorney/accountant/business advisor/health care partner/ethicist has done his or her job, a conflict or dispute may arise. The judicial system is too cumbersome, expensive, time-consuming and uncertain to persist. Alternative means of resolving disputes will dominate the scene. The litigator of the past will become the arbitrator, mediator or presenter to either. Knowledge of the law, the system, the procedure and the forms will no longer suffice.

Reflections on Marvin Fish

I don't expect any special favors from attorney Marvin Fish, although he is my personal attorney, as well as my friend. My reason for enclosing his remarks is the prestigious background of his professional work. He has been a professor, teaching ethics in universities, as well as working in the medical community teaching the problems, laws and ethics of the practice of medicine.

Fish has been instrumental as a consultant to me and my affairs. I cannot overlook one of the strangest lawsuits in history. For many years, I have held the position that the hypnotic trance does not exist. There is simply no such thing, whether performed on stage or in a medical setting. This is a position I have held for over 30 years. I contend that anything that is done under "hypnosis" can be done without it through persuasion and suggestion. I have demonstrated this contention around the world. The bottom line is that no matter whether anyone agrees with me or not, there isn't one trace of evidence that there is such a thing as a hypnotic state. To back my contention, I offered $50,000 to anyone who could prove my statement false. This was not some skeptic challenge to psychics. Those challenges are often not capable of being won because the conditions are such that the psychic would be a fool to take such a challenge. Mine would simply require a showing by psychological tests in an alter conscious state that what can be done legitimately under "hypnosis" cannot be done without it. No trick, no PR publicity challenge. If I wanted that, I would offer a billion dollars to anyone who could prove psychic phenomena with all its double-talk.

Finally, a few years ago, someone took on my challenge. That was fine with me. They would have the opportunity of demonstrating "hypnosis" before a clinical group and showing what they could do with a person hypnotized I could not do without the facade or illusion that someone is in a trance. After failing in the test, the hypnotist was not satisfied. She insisted on suing me. It is the only suit on record where the intent was to prove a hypnotic trance. The case was quickly thrown out of court on the second day. The judge said the hypnotist that brought the suit had wasted the time of the jury and the whole judicial arrangement. The hypnotist did not win the $50,000, but the case cost me $110,000. Without the counsel of Marvin Fish, I can only guess how much more it would have cost as it was a long, drawn out preparation for the case. I brought in mental and psychological witnesses who never had the chance to approach the witness stand. Incidentally, today I now offer $100,000 to anyone who can prove any kind of hypnotic trance, whether they do it on stage or in a medical setting. There is a catch this time, though, and I feel it is only fair to me. The person who accepts my challenge must agree to pay all expenses. I think I paid my dues in the courtroom.

The remarks of Marvin Fish, therefore, take on an even greater impact to me. Additionally, they will take on a greater impact to anyone who has some fear of becoming involved in a crazy lawsuit. If someone trips on the sidewalk in front of your house or they spill the coffee you gave them on their own arm they might sue you. There are people who have an insatiable need to avoid any personal responsibility. With that in mind, reread Mr. Fish's comments. He points out that in the years to come, it will not be enough for a lawyer to rest on his basic skills. He describes the need for truth, integrity, faithfulness, and reliability in our business and personal relationships. It is clear that, like the law enforcement officer, the attorney is going to have a working knowledge of psychology and ethics.

Fish's greatest reflection is the passage in which he states, "The judicial system is too cumbersome, expensive, time consuming and uncertain to persist." Let's hope he is correct in seeing the litigator of the past becoming an arbitrator. Wouldn't it be wonderful if that would be the first big step towards lessening the horrendous onslaught of lawsuits that just seem to plague our system and burden our courts. This is one of the prophesies I think we should all pray will come true.

BARRY BRANDMAN - Danbee Investigations

I anticipate that technology will have a significant impact in both the prevention and detection of business crime. Corporate sleuths will increase their use of extensive databases and specialized software programs that will provide a wealth of information when conducting fraud, embezzlement and due diligence investigations. I also foresee computers and closed circuit television systems becoming more efficiently integrated. Managers will have the ability to remotely oversee 10, 100 or even 1,000 satellite locations right from their laptops, which will provide an enhanced level of security and safety.

Reflections on Barry Brandman

I have been intrigued with the work of Barry Brandman ever since I met him on a flight some years ago. Brandman is the founder and president of Danbee Investigations, which is an organization that has devoted itself to preventing and detecting crime in the business scene. It is an area that much of the western world is unaware of. We hear a great deal about it in Russia, where suggestions are made that organized crime has a huge foothold on the government. The surveillance of criminal in the business setting is a difficult task and requires many varied techniques. I find fascinating Barry's prediction that with the proliferation of closed circuit televisions, managers can not only oversee multiple locations but that they can do so from their laptops!

I believe that we are now embroiled in the most unique war in modern history -- a war against terrorism. I wonder if these same techniques that Barry talks about can be used to fight the onslaught of this hidden enemy.

JOHN STOSSEL - ABC Television

Question: What do you foresee in the coming millennium regarding broadcasting and television? Answer: Beats me, but I will predict that, as usual, most predictions from the world's greatest entertainers, politicians, athletes, scientists, religious figures and humanitarians will be proven wrong!

Reflections on John Stossel

I asked John Stossel if he would reflect on his thoughts on the coming millennium. This remarkable news and television investigator has questioned some of the austere professions and their hierarchy. He has exposed some remarkable insight into medical and social activities. He seems to be in a position to have great insight into the broadcasting industry and the public conscious. I think his response to my question says it all.

ALEXANDER M. HAIG, Jr. - former Secretary of State

Dear Mr. Kreskin:

Thank you for your letter of August 3 requesting my thoughts on the next 1000 years or so. Unfortunately it would probably take me almost that long to compile my thoughts on this most weighty of subjects.

I would be grateful if you would accept my regrets. I am very flattered that you thought of me as a possible contributor for your important epic.

Sincerely,

Al Haig

Reflections on Alexander Haig

I had to include this most sincere letter from Alexander Haig although he declined to add his projections to this book. I am not sure, in truth, that he did not add to this volume in his own way. He mentions the time span of a 1000 years that it would take him to compile his thoughts. Does this suggest a sluggishness of thinking? Far from it. I think it suggests that his range of thoughts and concerns, and the depth with which he would need to examine them, would be extraordinarily extensive and myriad. In his own way he has made a rather refreshing contribution.

Sports

BRUCE JENNER -- OLYMPIC HERO

When Bruce Jenner won the Decathlon in the Olympics he was crowned the World's Greatest Athlete. He also became a national treasure. One of the country's favorite athletes of all time, he has enjoyed being a role model for kids and helping in charitable activities. One of his personal favorite honors was his appearance on the Wheaties cereal box, an honor that has come to mean you are a true champion. We quickly asked Bruce about upcoming Olympics.

Q: In the first Olympics of the millennium, who will win the most golds?

A: I'm a little biased - the US!

Q: Which sports will the US excel in?

A: We stay fairly competitive, if not at the top, of most sports.

Q: Not the luge, for instance.

A: Maybe I'll try that. I've been looking for a way back into competition.

Bruce, very patriotically, predicted the United States would win the most Gold Medals at the next Olympic Games. He also jokingly indicated that he might join the luge team to help the US chances in that event.

Reflections on Bruce Jenner

Jenner's quick comments are not groundbreaking for this book, nor does he have much to say about the millennium. However, it is nice to spotlight an athlete who deserves to be called a champion. Bruce has always projected a positive image and is a great role model for children. I just don't see him as the type of person who would get in fights in night clubs, run down people crossing the street or ignoring kids who ask for an autograph. Refreshingly, Mr. Jenner has enjoyed his role model status.

As for professional sports today, I feel some disappointment. The attitudes of players has changed drastically in recent years, and they seem to lose perspective. Sports is a game, and the fan wants to enjoy it for the game. The greedy athlete and the greedy sports franchise owner have made the field of sports a business and the fans don't like it. The fans want to see it played for the love of the game. That is why the Olympics are so popular. Certainly there is big money involved in the Olympics, but the money is not going to the athletes. They compete for the glory of the sport. After the Olympic games of 1996, 1 was asked who I thought was the epitome of the true Olympian. My choice at the time was Andre Agassi, the tennis pro. Throughout his career he had won nearly every major tennis tournament one could imagine and made a huge amount of money. But in the spirit of the Olympics he played for no compensation. He played for the glory of the game and to bring honor to the United States. Andre Agassi brought home the Gold medal.

Today, the modern sports player needs to take a look at his predecessors and remember why he got into the sport in the first place -- a love of the game.

MAGIC JOHNSON - Basketball Legend

As one of the top fifty basketball players of all time, Magic Johnson place in basketball's Hall of Fame is assured. He rounded out his career by representing the United States on the Dream Team basketball team that won the gold medal at the Olympics. He has coached the Los Angeles Lakers and hosted his own television show, The Magic Hour. He retired from basketball while he was in his prime shortly after being diagnosed as HIV positive. We ran into him on the set of his television show.

Q: Do you think a cure for HIV will be found in the coming century?

A: Getting deep on me, huh?

Q: Just interested in your opinion.

A: I hope it doesn't take that long.

Q: So you think certainly in the coming millennium?

A: I can only hope, but I would say "yes".

Q: With all the fundraisers and awareness, why hasn't a cure been found?

A: If it was easy, I'm sure there would be a cure. Researchers and other people are working hard, it takes time.

Q: If a cure is found, do you think it will be available only to those with money?

A: That's, I mean, no, man. If there is a cure, the people who need it will get it.

Magic Johnson has worked hard to increase HIV awareness and offers hope to the sick and underprivileged. He predicts a cure for HIV will be found and that its availability will be without limits.

Reflections on Magic Johnson

You will note that Johnson was interviewed on the set of his television show, so it is understandable that the interview was so brief -- his television show was just a flash of light, or a spark that ran out almost instantly. Even this short interview suggests that Magic Johnson is much better at basketball than he is as a talk show host.

He is truly an inspiration in the sports world and he is to be admired for his courage in publicly acknowledging his HIV diagnosis. He is also to be admired for his determination to raise awareness for the disease and to help find a cure. It is best that we forget that someone convinced him to be the host of his own talk show. He is a victim along with scores of others who between now and the next millennium will be convinced that having watched television they can simply go on to be a success as a talk show host. It is reaching a point where television is suffering from verbal diarrhea.

ANDRE AGASSI -- Tennis Player

Andre Agassi is one of the most successful tennis players of all time. His success on the court has translated to success off the court, as he is the spokesman for many national products. He has won major tournaments, been ranked number one in the world and is very flashy. Incidentally, he is married to Brooke Sheilds. We spoke with Andre about trends in his sport.

Q: Do you see any tends in the sport in the coming millennium?

A: The age of the top new tennis players has been dropping like a rock. I don't think it will continue to go lower. I think the trend might even move towards higher.

Q: The new stars will emerge at a later age?

A: They can't get much younger. Players are turning pro at 15, 16, sometimes younger. I don't think the trend down can continue. The strength won't be there, and coaches are seeing that burn out can destroy a career that starts that early.

Q: So coaches will keep players from turning pro until they reach an older age.

A: I hope so. It would be good for them and the game.

Q: How do you think the US will do in Davis Cup in the next millennium?

A: American tennis is healthy, we will continue to win.

Q: Any interest in becoming the coach?

A: I'd have to stand in line behind McEnroe.

Reflections on Andre Agassi

There are many interesting issues raised in Agassi's remarks. He talks about the trend in tennis for players to emerge on the scene at such an early age that they can burn out quickly and destroy a promising career. This same situation has happened in other areas as well. I have seen high school students ruined by overzealous coaches. These players, who had dreams of building a professional football career, were ruined before they enter college. It is a very mature perspective that Agassi has shown in examining his sport.

It can be argued that in recent years tennis' popularity has receded. This may because of the competition for attention from other sports, but it is probably because of a lack of a dynamic player who brings skills and enthusiasm to the game that surpass simply hitting a ball. With Andre injured and out of the spotlight, the sport missed his energy and style. The qualities that Agassi displays, while indefinable, will eventually show up in a future player, who will again bring the spotlight back to the world of tennis.

I have never been a sports fan, but I became acutely aware of the sport of tennis while in England. Later that night I was to perform my show, but during the day I was watching a match in which John McEnroe was playing. In an episode that was certainly not unusual, McEnroe became upset with the decision of one of the judges and began spewing obscenities. As I sat there, as an American guest in the country, where audiences were about to see me, I squirmed as another American behaved so badly. McEnroe's antics brought great attention to the sport, and for some who are only concerned with the bottom line, that was enough. However, it was one of the most embarrassing days of my life.

WHITEY FORD - Baseball Hall Of Famer

I can't see salaries going any higher and baseball being able to stay in business. The players have gotten the most money possible. Owners would be financially irresponsible to spend more on salaries.

There will be no more expansion in baseball. The game has grown about as much as it can. The talent level has already been diluted by expansion. A good example of this is the real lack of overall outstanding pitching as there was when I played.

The popularity of baseball will recover. Hopefully both sides learned their lesson with the last strike.

Reflections on Whitey Ford

I really hope that Whitey Ford's comments about the future of baseball have hit a home run. In this past year, with the breaking of the homerun record, positive attention and fan support returned to baseball. The conflicts between the millionaire players and the billionaire owners were forgotten and the public cheered for the purity of the sport. It took a historic race for the homerun record to bring back the romance of baseball. In the back of my mind I can still hear the voice of Mel Allen who had an incredibly romantic way of commenting on the baseball scene. I have never been much of a sports fan, but I marveled at Mel's ability to mesmerize an audience while he told stories of the world of baseball while he stalled during rain delays that could last over an hour. My father and brother would sit glued to the radio listening to his commentary. There aren't many sports reporters today who could maintain the interest of the listeners as well as Mel Allen did.

I am intrigued at how values have changed and how the perspective is warped for the younger kids today. I remember a time when boys and girls traded baseball cards. Today, those cards are kept encased in plastic in hopes of selling them for a profit at a later date. The innocence and fun of the game has been somewhat lost. Of course there is still romance to this leisurely game of baseball. It almost has the fragrance of Hoagy Carmichael's "Stardust."

I am pleased that Whitey Ford made this contribution.

MIKE PIAZZA -- Baseball Player

Mike Piazza is arguably baseball's best player, and certainly one of its highest paid We asked Mike a number of baseball questions.

Q: Do you see any major trends or changes in baseball in the coming millennium?

A: Like what?

Q: Do you think the designated hitter will stay?

A: Probably -- the Player's Union wants it. It's not going anywhere.

Q: Do you see any changes in baseball at all?

A: What are you getting at?

Q: I'm just interested in whether you have any opinions or predictions about trends in baseball.

A: Well, for one thing, the game is getting much more diverse. We're seeing guys like Nomo, Irabu, Hernandez, guys like that. Scouting is increasing in other areas.

Q: Do you think scouting will continue in other countries, then?

A: Sure. As long as the scouts are finding places with talent, they'll keep looking there and keep signing people.

Q: You're about to sign a $100 million dollar deal at the end of the season -- who do you think will sign you?

A: I have no idea.

Q: Do you have any preferences?

A: I want to play for a winner, and I want to be able to make a contribution.

Q: So, if you want a winner, the Yankees look like a good bet, they have money and they need a catcher.

A: Who knows. No teams can talk to me during the season -- it's tampering.

Q: How many years do you think it will take for the new expansion teams, say the Arizona Diamondbacks, to win the World Series?

A: It depends on what players they get and how they develop their team. Arizona has a great manager -- Buck -- and if they get enough talent, they can win immediately -- look at the Marlins. Didn't take them long.

Q: Let's pin down a prediction. Can the Diamondbacks win the World Series within ten years?

A: Certainly. It all depends on the team and Buck knows how to put together a team.

Mike didn't have any predictions as to where he will play next year, but he did feel that the game has become more multi-national. He mentioned two Japanese pitchers - Nomo and Irabu, and a Cuban pitcher - Hernandez. Mike predicted that the scouts will continue to look to other countries for baseball prospects. Mike also predicted that the expansion teams can make an impact quickly and could possibly win the World Series soon after the turn of the millennium.

Reflections on Mike Piazza

Howard Cosell once said that the scope of conversation of a baseball player can only be appreciated when one realizes that baseball players sit for hours in a dugout where they see an extraordinarily narrowed horizon. They in essence have a very limited picture of the world. It is refreshing to see that some of the sports figures interviewed for this book have widened their perspective by communicating with others outside of their area of expertise.

Certainly, Piazza is one of baseball's best players and it is refreshing to hear his comments. While he comments that the game is becoming more multi-national and teams are scouting in foreign countries, it worries me that players are becoming less likely to stay on a team. Players seem to jump from team to team and money seems to be the only factor. I hope this trend reverses.

STEVE GARVEY -- Baseball Player

Q: Do you think Pete Rose belongs in the Hall of Fame?

A: Do you?

Q: He sure got a lot of hits.

A: I think that sums it up.

Q: Do you think he will get in.

A: Sure, eventually.

Q: Do you see any trends emerging in the game?

A: It's becoming much more of a business. It would be nice to see teams play more for the game, for enjoyment, rather than money.

Q: What about salaries, will they continue to spiral?

A: I think the owners will try to implement some type of a salary cap.

Q: Who will be the most dominant team in the next millennium?

A: That's a ways off. Next couple of years certainly looks like the Yankees.

Reflections on Steve Garvey

Steve Garvey became famous as a member of the World Champion Dodger teams of the early eighties. He had a remarkable baseball career and played on a number of championship teams. He also became a best-selling author when he wrote his autobiography.

His response about Pete Rose was interesting. Pete Rose, who holds the record for the most hits ever in baseball, was banned for life from the game for gambling. There has been a huge controversy about his ineligibility for the Hall of Fame due to his ban. Many say that it is incredulous to not have the record holder for hits in the Hall, while others say that he brought his punishment on himself and he reaps what he sows. Steve Garvey seems to say Rose has earned the right to be in the Hall and predicted that Pete Rose will eventually be elected to enter.

My gut feeling is that Pete Rose will never find his way into the Hall of Fame. I also feel he in no way earned the right to enter. His gambling habits are legendary, even at the race tracks in Florida. I don't think we need to absolve a person of his responsibility.

Steve Garvey also predicted that the owners will implement some type of salary cap and that the Yankees will be the team to beat the next few years.

TOMMY LASORDA -- Baseball Manager

As one of baseballs best known managers, Tommy Lasorda is a legend in the game. He managed the Los Angeles Dodgers for over twenty years and was on the field for many of that franchises most memorable moments. He is an expert in all things baseball. We were able to speak with Tommy at Dodger Stadium recently.

Q: Do you think players' salaries will continue to skyrocket in the coming century?

A: Salaries need to be solved now. The salaries are becoming out of control. Kids are being signed to million dollar contracts -- without one day of major league experience. Salaries should be earned -- on the field.

Q: How can owners afford the salaries if they keep going up, even if they are earned on the field?

A: Baseball is a business. The owners add up their expenses and try to make a profit. Salaries are an expense. If the salaries keep rising, the owners will have to make more money -- and the fix includes raising ticket prices. It is sad to see a family of four having to pay $100 to enjoy a baseball game.

Q: With television paying huge amounts to air games, and new revenue sources, like play-by-play on the Internet, couldn't owners make there money elsewhere, and leave the fans with cheaper tickets?

A: The Internet is a source of income?

Q: Sure, ESPN just paid millions for the right o broadcast games pitch by pitch over the internet.

A: I didn't know that. That's interesting. What was the question?

Q: With these added sources of revenue, couldn't ticket prices remain where they are?

A: That makes sense, but they do keep rising.

Tommy didn't see any end in sight for escalating player salaries. In a year when new player contracts will top $100 million dollars, Tommy's prediction of no end in sight is scary. He also predicted that ticket prices would continue to rise to help defray player salary costs even though baseball owners are making money through alternative sources.

Reflections on Tommy Lasorda

With Tommy Lasorda we once more hear the ominous prediction that salaries will continue to skyrocket into the coming century. Lasorda agrees that the salaries are out of control. It is a rather intriguing observation when he points out that kids are being signed to million dollar contracts without a day of Major League experience. Is this what we want to reflect to the youth of America? This seems to show them that it is not necessary to earn or prove oneself worthy of such a high salary. Lasorda mentions that baseball is a business, and perhaps I can expand on his remark. Sports today is show business and show business consists of two words. People often forget the second word is business.

BENJAMIN LUNTZ -- Physicist

In the last half of the twentieth century there has been a great intermixing of ideas and concepts between the East and West. One area the West has enthusiastically embraced is the martial arts. An active martial arts tradition has been established in the West and this tradition should continue to grow well into the next century. For children and adolescents, we can expect to see recreational martial arts become as common as traditional western sports such as baseball or basketball. Among adults and the elderly, we shall see the slow moving forms like Tai Chi Chuan practiced in ever increasing numbers. Just as the Chinese have benefited from the physical and psychological effects of Tai Chi Chuan, so shall Americans benefit in the twenty-first century.

On a more general level, the basic philosophical viewpoints of the East and West have and will continue to be exchanged. To give a simplified example of this, note that we in the West have tended to view things in terms of their parts rather than seeing them as a whole. On the other hand, people in the East have tended to view things as a whole rather than in terms of their parts. There are advantages and disadvantages to both these points of view. With the practical intermixing of these different perspectives, these two civilizations can look forward to enjoying the advantages of both.

In regard to the more advanced aspects of the martial arts, the next century will be a time of rediscovery in which at least some of the unusual abilities possessed by past masters will be redeveloped. With this redevelopment will come a deeper understanding of the physical, physiological, and psychological mechanisms that underlie these unusual abilities. Kreskin's many insights into the unconscious, his explanation of hyper-esthesia, and his methods of achieving hyper-esthesia, all taken together, will be the foundation of this future redevelopment and understanding of unusual abilities in the martial arts.

Reflections on Benjamin Luntz

Benjamin Luntz is a unique man, trained with a Doctorate in Theoretical Nuclear Physics and a seriously trained martial artist. He has written a book that has given me great personal satisfaction, "Martial Arts: Science and Mysticism." I thoroughly enjoyed it and believe it is a great book for anyone interested in the discipline and the potential. It was a personal delight to find that many of the concepts in his book originated from my writings and those of Carl Sagan. What Luntz attempted to do was scientifically explain some of the unusual abilities found in the martial arts field. These explanations were to help the martial arts become more understandable and acceptable to the Western World.

His millennium predictions are very interesting. He points out that not only will martial arts gain popularity with mainstream adults, but they will touch the lives of children and the elderly. He points to the benefits the Chinese have seen, such as physical and psychological health.

It is intriguing to read his insight on how the West views things as compared to our counterparts in the East. I have thought about this over the years and can clearly see pluses and minus to the way each culture thinks and acts. It is clear that by sharing concepts the benefits of both perspectives can be realized. I would like to think that Benjamin Luntz has the communication ability and intriguing philosophies in his writings to bring the East closer to the West, and the West closer to the East. This ideal of mixing both perspectives must inevitably become a fulfillment.

SHIFU ROBERT REDIFEATHER - Master of Tie

Gou Quan Shaolin Boxing

It is difficult to predict what the future holds, and trying to predict as far out in time as a thousand years is nearly impossible. However, there are a number of trends that lead to the belief that the following will come to pass in the new millennium.

1.   The martial arts will all combine into one style. Hundreds of years ago in Tibet, the martial arts began as a form of exercise and meditation and developed into a fighting art form. As experts in the skill migrated to other lands, they began to name their particular style after themselves. The first geographic area to make an impact with new styles was China and Japan, and soon other far eastern countries began developing their own styles. Today, there are hundreds of martial art styles, and as the next century comes to a close, a major trend in the consolidation of these styles will have taken root and eventually, the martial arts will consists of one main style.

2.   Martial artists take advantage of their environment and use their surroundings in their techniques. As space exploration becomes more commonplace, colonization on other planets is inevitable. As a result, new techniques will be developed to take advantage of environmental differences found on other planets. For example, techniques that leverage new gravitational climates will be perfected.

3.   Similarly to the consolidation of martial arts styles, city police departments will be engulfed into a nationwide police department. This will streamline information sharing and standardized policies. No longer will there be a Los Angeles Police Department and a New York Police Department, etc. There will be the United States Sheriffs, and they will have substations across the land.

Reflections on Shifu Robert Redfeather

The comments by Robert Redfeather are intriguing. It is very interesting to see someone in the martial arts field thinking about the implications of space travel on their craft. However, Robert Redfeather's incredibly diverse background gives insight into how he thinks. In addition to his mastery in the martial arts field he has previously been a professional bull rider as well as a bounty hunter. He currently runs martial arts studios on the West Coast. As a result of his interesting life experience, it is not unusual to see him pondering life's most exciting questions.

It certainly seems accurate that as colonization of other planets occurs, that martial arts will evolve to incorporate the new environment. I'm sure Redfeather will be one of the leaders of the development of martial arts in these new frontiers.

GRAND MASTER CLIFFORD C. CRANDALL, JR. - martial artist

Where are sports going tomorrow, next week or next year? To understand the direction of sports in the future we need to look first and foremost at the competitors. The competitive spirit of the human being, combined with the increased mental and emotional pressure of today's world, is pushing sports to a new limit every year.

Excellent athletes are actually adrenaline and goal junkies encouraged and used by the crowds and trainers. They are only a few in number, but their personal need to feel life through the risk of losing it keeps them fulfilled and happy. But as they challenge this drive, they open a door for others to follow. Many people seek the challenge and risk, but need the odds to be slightly, if not comfortably, in their favor. Once one of the few has proven it can be done, and in turn demonstrates the unknown can be known before you try it yourself, the door is open and others will follow. Like the cutting edge of computer technology, so too is the process of sports and the challenge to truly live life.

As a result, sports are drifting from the concept of the team to the individual. In short, the success of one person above all has become the key to tomorrow's sports. Team players are now singled out as the key player or most valuable player. News coverage shows the play of the day or the highest paid player's statistics. This is leading to lack of sportsmanship, the acceptance of fights and aggressive actions between athletes even of the same team. These outbursts include swearing, violent hand gestures, physical fighting and the use of chairs as weapons. The audience has become more interested in the level of risk to life and well being than achievement and success.

Is this all bad or good, and what will it lead to? Can it be changed? Or better yet, should this direction be changed?

The future holds an increased level of individual challenges. Sports will become more focused on the level of difficulty and risk to participants as paramount for whether or not the sport is interesting. The hard and true sports, like the oldies but goodies radio shows, will stay alive much like the appreciation of the old cars and classic motorcycles. But the new sports will definitely be on the edge of technology and physical ability. Injuries will become accepted, as legal waivers will become more complete and binding. In most new sports to come, speed will become a key factor, even in martial arts. The level of acrobatics and speed will increase in forms and sparring. The new era of martial arts will truly become exhibition oriented and leave the traditional foundation of loyalty, self-control and harmony, which were the original reasons for the martial arts. The key will be not so much to prevent this growing change in direction but to keep alive the original concepts of the martial arts and other sports. The pendulum will swing back and it is important that when it does there is enough remaining of the philosophy of good sportsmanship, teamwork, personal pride, and safety to allow these qualities to be used again.

Reflections on Clifford C. Crandall, Jr.

Clifford Crandall is one of the most dynamic figures in the Martial Arts field in the Western World. In addition to writing the acclaimed martial arts textbook, "American Eagle Style", he has appeared on network television shows and major news broadcasts performing dramatic feats. His physical abilities are impressive, but his analysis of the trends in sports that fascinates me immensely. I have never been a big spectator sports fan, but I have been concerned with the erosion of the spirit of sports. It is as if the dollar sign has become more important than the very spirit of competitive playing. Crandall's remarks are dramatic because it doesn't matter what sport you love to watch or play, his views touch home. He has highlighted the fact that the focus of attention these days is on the key players and highest paid players -- at the sacrifice of the team. His philosophical and spiritual concerns not only deal with sports, but with the game of life.

Health & Science

DR JOYCE BROTHERS - Noted Psychologist

Q: I am creating a book that investigates what changes experts in a variety of fields see for the coming millennium. How do you see the world of psychology, either clinical or counseling, will change in the next century?

A: I am sure that we are going to find a physiological basis for the serious mental problems -schizophrenia, bipolar disorders -- disorders of that kind. Many years ago, during my training, I prepared a report, pulling together what little research had been done to date, on the concept that schizophrenia might be a physiological disorder.

Q: There was very little indication suggesting it?

A: There was very little, but there was some. At that time there was the concept that the psychologists should live with the family of the patient a little bit. They could deal with the family dynamics that might be causal to the schizophrenia. I said, "No, it is much more physiological." I received a "C" on my paper -- the only "C" I ever received in my life. Years later I got a letter from my professor saying "Here's the W. I owe you."

Q: Well, look at alcoholism today. The perspective there has really changed.

A: I think that in the future many more psychiatrists and psychologists will need biochemistry as the bedrock of their training. We will not dispense with the emotional and psychological areas, although there will be a need for the ability to deal with these disorders on the basis of medication or even gene manipulation. There will always be the need for face to face "how do we make my life better and smoother" that can only occur in the office of a psychologist.

Q: There seems to be an undercurrent in the opinions of people, even those not in behavioral areas, that the computer is affecting the way people relate to each other. Do you have any thoughts?

A: Well, I really think that in the future the computer will be like our telephone -- where people take it for granted. I don't think it will change relationships drastically. For instance, just because the computer can help children learn, and there is immediate feedback on schoolwork, the need for teachers will not be eliminated. We need that human to human touch. So, relationships won't change drastically, but computers will help us make diagnosis in the medical fields much easier. Physicians can send the EEG's and other diagnostic reading via computer.

Q: Incredible.

A: And that has helped in the diagnosis, but you still need to go to a specialist to read the diagnostics. For me, I believe the computer will simply be a helping hand. It won't in anyway interfere with the ability to think and reason as a human being.

Q: That is the most positive response I have heard. How do you think the loss of privacy will change our world in the years to come?

A: It may be better. We are losing our privacy, but at the same time we are losing our ability to skirt things.

Q: I have always felt that the last thing a man has is his thoughts. If we an find out everything about our neighbors, how can we live like that?

A: You handle living like that by living honestly and openly and by really living by the Ten Commandments -- with a lack of privacy you won't have an opportunity to bend them.

Q: What a refreshing commentary.

Reflections on Dr. Joyce Brothers

I cannot imagine psychologist, Dr. Joyce Brothers, not being part of the communication scene in our culture. From the days when she would comment on various aspects of human behavior on her own NBC television program to the years she spent answering telephone calls of troubled or inquisitive listeners on radio, Dr. Brothers has been a mainstay in broadcasting. She has been an important part of modern communications. I remember quite well the day she kept a suicidal caller talking, on the air, long enough for help to arrive at the caller's location. Throughout her years of television and radio communications and her brilliant writings, she has kept a sense of humor that reveals that she is not only a psychologist, but a showman as well. I appeared recently with her on the Howard Stern radio and television show to play Howard's own version of Jeopardy. Stern was trying to prepare Robin Quivers, his brilliant partner, for an appearance on the Jeopardy television series. Dr. Brothers was right at home, contributing to the comedy as well as showing us her unquestionable brilliance. What I think is most remarkable about the advice she gives to listeners is her incredible reservoir of knowledge. She is invariably able to refer to a piece of research or the comments of a prominent therapist on the very topic the caller is asking about. Dr. Brothers has as close to a true photographic memory as one can imagine. I have heard the story a dozen times by people in the field of the time when Dr. Brothers was challenged to a memory test and successfully memorized, in order, 101 digits. She is truly remarkable.

BUZZ ALDREN -- Astronaut

Q: Do you think we'll land a man on Mars in the next millennium?

A: Yes.

Q: Does the space program have the technology or funding for it?

A: NASA is hugely popular. The space shuttle program has been incredibly successful and generated huge popularity. The money won't be a problem.

Q: How about colonizing the moon?

A: There might be a space station built on the moon, where testing can take place.

Reflections on Buzz Aldren

The remarks of Buzz Aldren interested me immensely. There aren't many professions that are as admired in our culture as astronaut. Children love to dream about their chance to become a space traveler, and adults feel the admiration of those men that wear the US flag on their suit as they hurl towards other planets. Aldren's place in history is well established. He is a legend in the space program and has walked on the moon.

His thoughts about space and the next millennium intrigued me for personal reasons. Some years ago, Edgar Mitchell, one of our outstanding astronauts, quietly conducted a telepathy test while hurling through space on a dramatic mission that had the world watching. When his telepathy test became public, he admirably offered no apologies. He had a great interest in certain areas of ESP. After the mission, he saw one of my appearances on the Johnny Carson show and sent me a beautiful complimentary letter, which I read on national television. Mitchell and I planned a meeting in Texas. I wanted to discuss some concerns I had for him as parapsychology was new to him and I worried that he could become involved in people or sources that might take advantage of his enthusiasm. I wanted to provide some illumination about some of the bad apples. The appointment was never kept. He did not show up and I was most disappointed.

I would like to offer to conduct a telepathy test between myself and one of the astronauts on the next major space flight. It would be exciting and interesting to see the extent of success that we could achieve using telepathy over such a vast distance.

DR. LUCY JONES - Earthquake Specialist

Dr. Lucy Jones is one of the nation's foremost earthquake specialists. She is called upon by most major media outlets to report and analyze earthquakes whenever an event occurs in California, and elsewhere. We had the opportunity to ask her about her predictions for the possibility of upcoming earthquakes.

Q: Will there be a massive earthquake in the coming century?

A: It certainly is probable. The research and data all say we are due. Exactly when is the question and we could be decades away.

Q: If the "Big One" hits, will it be like in the movies, with California breaking off and becoming an island and Arizona having beachfront property?

A: It's possible that a massive initial quake could cause some breakoff, but more than likely you would see on-land property destruction like the San Francisco quake.

Happily for those in California, Dr. Jones doesn't predict California will break off from the rest of the country after a large earthquake. She does predict a big quake is coming in the next century, but feels the damage will be to property, not land.

Reflections on Dr. Lucy Jones

Dr. Lucy Jones works for Cal Tech as an earthquake specialist and is called in by the media whenever California is hit with an earthquake. I happen to have been in the city during one of the earthquakes. Fortunately for me, it was not one of California's largest of the past decade. Even so, I was lying on my bed in a suite on the top floor of a hotel and thought the building had been hit by an airplane. The electricity went out and my shades were drawn, so I found myself crawling on the floor over to the window, where I pulled up the shades to let daylight into the room. I knew something dramatic had happened as I could see hundreds of people running from the building. It was an unforgettable experience.

While Dr. Jones feels that the damage will be to property, not land, the more serious conjecture is the amount of harm to people. I was told by authorities in California that a serious quake could injure over a million people! The dilemma is that even if we develop an early warning system, it will be hard to help people. We do not live in a dictatorship and so we cannot simply order people out of a city to protect them from Mother Nature. How to overcome this dilemma is something that has frustrated authorities for years.

DR. EDWARD TELLER - developed the Atomic Bomb

In physics, real changes are few and far between. After the Greeks, there have been two great changes:

1.   Sixteenth/Seventeenth Century: Copernicus and Galileo - the earth is not the center of the universe.

2.   Twentieth Century: Einstein/Bohr - Relativity and Quantum Mechanics

No one can predict when the next change will come and what it will be, especially because of today's distrust of science. My sincere hope is that this feeling will not continue.

What I hope for is that by the Year 3000, we will understand, to some extent, what life is.

Reflections on Dr. Edward Teller

I received this communication, from the world-renowned physicist Dr. Edward Teller, from the Hoover Institute. The Hoover Institution exists on the theme of war and peace. With that in mind, I find it fascinating that Dr. Teller finds the distrust in science to be holding back advances. For years, attorneys and politicians were treated with a measure of distrust, and now scientists are being placed in this category. Have we become distrustful because of recent findings that scientific research could be altered to suit the special interest groups behind the studies? Or, is it because there is a feeling that scientists are personally motivated to achieve certain ends? Or, is it possibly the years of exposure to science fiction writers who have warned us of the abuses of science, as in Mary Shelley's Frankenstein. It is certainly something to reflect upon and yet there is no question that the greatest advances of life will be found through the scientists.

DEBRA W. HAFFNER - Human Sexuality

Sexuality will finally be recognized as a natural and central part of life. All parents will have the skills to provide sexuality education from early childhood through adolescence. All schools, churches and synagogues, and community-based organizations will have sexuality education programs from children and youth. The media will recognize and respect its role in providing information about sexuality to people of all ages. The Internet will be a source of highly accurate, non-exploitative information about sexuality at all stages of life. We will like our bodies, have respectful relationships with people of both genders, and have meaningful lifelong intimate relationships. Gays and lesbians will be able to marry and live without violence and discrimination. All children will be wanted and we will be immunized at birth against all sexually transmitted diseases. AIDS will be eradicated.

Amen!

Reflections on Debra W. Haffner

Ms. Haffner is President and CEO of The Sexuality Information and Education Council of the United States. I find her most remarkable prediction for the millennium is that parents will have the skills to provide sexual education to their children from early childhood through adolescence. This would be a much-welcomed development. For decades, society has left much of this education in the hands of various churches, schools and public groups -- all of which are lacking the rapport and closeness that is inherent between a parent and child. It is also refreshing to hear of Debra's prediction that the Internet will be a source of accurate and **non-exploitive** information. Perhaps we are beginning to see the great potential the Internet has been promising. Finally, while it is hard to believe today, I agree with her powerful prediction that "AIDS will be eradicated!"

DIAN WILLIAMS - ARSON RESEARCH

Mr. Kreskin: I must confess to feeling somewhat bemused at your description of me as one of "arson prevention's greatest legends" which makes me sound either like I'm 400 years old or that I should be playing piano in a smoke-filled little jazz club somewhere! Nevertheless, I will take the opportunity to consider the next millennium and arson.

We must, as a society, come to terms with the understanding that children and adolescents who set fires often do so as an expression of rage and frustration. As we look into the future, it is vital to recognize that children have taken on increased responsibility to raise themselves and have done the best that children could do with the task. Unfortunately, raising children takes parents, and other extended members of the family and the community. I fear children over the next millennium will take on even more responsibility and perhaps childhood will be a thing of the past. As it is, childhood was an invention of the 20th century and I believe adults have run out of patience for it.

I believe that children over the next millennium will be exposed to too much responsibility too soon and will suffer as a result. Children will be increasingly exposed to scenes of violence at home and in school. Firesetting and firebombing behavior will increase as children become acclimated to the use of violent and dangerous behavior as a method of self-expression.

Only if our society recognizes the impact of poor parenting, lack of appropriate attention and treatment and the effects on children of witnessing violence do we have the possibility of escape from such a dire prediction.

Reflections on Dian Williams

I found the remarks of Dian Williams, President and CEO of Arson Research, absolutely intriguing and I have reread them a number of times. They are a fascinating commentary on society. She discusses the assumption that children have taken on the task of raising themselves, and the fear that in the next millennium they will have to take on even more responsibility. She comments that 11 childhood will be a thing of the past." It is a true commentary that childhood is an invention of the 20th century, as children in past centuries were forced into adulthood much before they reached their teens. Read the writings of Charles Dickens and you will understand further another period in our history. It is a commentary that needs to be reflected upon - especially when you note the remarks that dangerous behavior is a method of self expression. I consider this entry to be one of the most important of my entire book - it warrants much reflection.

RAYMOND PORTER -- Natural Gas Expert

The exploration for natural gas reservoirs has become of increased significance in the field of energy in proportion to the National Energy Reserves. There should be an increasing demand for the environmentally safe reliable source of natural gas as a clean burning motor fuel particularly in view of the foreign oil producing countries' unpredictability. As heating oil prices increase, more heating systems, particularly in the northeastern quadrant of the US, will be converted to the cleaner burning natural gas. Also, electric power generating plants will continue to be converted to natural gas to eliminate the atmospheric pollution of heavy fuel oils and coal. Natural gas engine driven heat pump air conditioning systems will become more prevalent for commercial, industrial, and residential usage.

This increased usage will require additional large pipelines for the transportation of natural gas from the well production collector systems to this expanding market. Unitary prices for natural gas at the well head should remain favorable or increase in relation to the exploration cost. This will enable the Wildcat exploration and drilling speculators to continue in the highly risky gamble in the quest for new sources well into the next millennium.

In the early days of Wildcatting for oil fields, natural gas was a nuisance to the oil producer, a byproduct to be burned or flared off as a means of disposal. Ultimately gas lines began to be laid for distribution to user locations and the gas light era came into being.

If natural gas continues to increase in demand in the next 100 years, as it has in the past, it will by necessity bring new technological developments to aid in improved methods of locating the reservoirs and reduce the risk for the exploration operators.

Reflections on Raymond Porter

I consider Ray Porter a life-long friend and I value his commentary because of his remarkable life experiences. Over the years he has been successful in a diverse array of activities, from designing air conditioning units which found their way into homes and cars, to piloting planes. He currently has ongoing business dealings with foreign sources, including Japan. He remains a fascinating character with a most incredible sense of humor. I can remember his recounting of the time he saw the late Henny Youngman perform at a dinner show. Unfortunately for Henny, he had to perform his legendary routines while the people where still dining, occupied with their food and drink. It is one of the horrendous moments that every performer dreads. Porter recognized the situation and decided to help Henny. Porter left his table, pulled his chair up to the stage, put his feet up on the stage, crossed his arms and looked glaringly at Youngman. This opened an avenue of commentary from Youngman, with Porter responding. People stopped. Their surprise moved to a hushed attentiveness in order to see what was going on between the two apparent antagonists. Within a short time the audience was filled with laughter as people now started to hear the repertoire of Henny Youngman. After the show, Youngman had a drink with Porter and thanked him for saving his neck in such a difficult situation.

Porter is also very persuasive. I have always had a fear of heights, but when Ray Porter became an aficionado of ballooning as well as a safety official in the organization of balloonists, I soon found myself hovering above the clouds in awe of the tremendous quiet one experiences sitting in the basket of a hot air balloon. My most memorable part of the ride came from the fact that as one hovers over the earth, you can hear conversations of people who are simply speaking a normal level of volume as they walk on the ground.

There seems to be no end to this man's search of adventure, even in the business world. In recent years, I have found him to be searching for hidden gas reservoirs. His reflections predict this will be a source of energy in the future. I grew up knowing that people searched for oil and now this Texas gentleman has taken the search to natural gas, the cleaner and potentially important new step.

GERARD V. SUNNEN, M.D. -- The Science of the Mind

As time soars into the third millennium, we intuitively realize that our lives will never be the same. The coming transformations affecting all domains of earthly life will have a direct impact upon fundamental notions concerning our existence and our innermost nature.

Strikingly pivotal, the 20th century has altered our essential view of our outer world - the earth and its ambient cosmos - and our inner world, the mind itself. In this transition from one millennium to the next, psychiatry, the nascent science of the mind, is following a sharp ascendant trajectory in its culmination of discoveries and advances.

At the beginning of our 20th century, psychiatry stood alone as a renegade and frankly stigmatized discipline; it has now forged increasingly intricate connections to all known sciences, from neurology and biochemistry, to sociology, and even to atomic physics. If psychiatry is conceived as a science giving birth at the time of the new millennium, it will be doing so to novel and exhilarating concepts about the mind which, like the clearing of a fog, will allow an endless rainbow of new possibilities to show its brilliant colors.

Three such concepts deserve special attention. One has to do with the psyche's close interdependence with neuro-chemical events within the brain. The other concerns the important role neuronal genes have upon all mental expression - from mood to behavior. The third and by far the most elusive is interested in the relationship of the mind to the actual physical matter of the nervous system.

Within the last two decades, the capacity to picture events occurring in the brain, non-invasively and without discomfort to individuals, has grown remarkably in its sophistication and precision.

Freud himself stated that one day every thought would be physically traced in the brain at the moment of its occurrence. That time has come. The brain is showing its color-coded maps in even greater detail, and the pathways of its circuits in ever finer minutiae. Neuro-chemicals responsible for sustaining brain/mind functions are increasingly yielding their identities. Their sheer numbers and role in contributing to common psychiatric conditions are constantly catalogued and elucidated.

Awaiting us is a psychiatry armed with an army of highly specific medications geared to the particular condition afflicting the unique individual involved. This pinpoint accuracy will revolutionize the therapy of all mental disturbances. Serious long-standing depressions, for example, could foreseeably be treated by the administration of rapid treatments resulting in a quasi-instantaneous resolution of all symptoms.

The "New Psychopharmacology" is poised to offer potent instruments for humanity's gravest psychiatric ills. In counterpoint, it will be applied to enhance already "normal" mental states by encouraging the expression of such vital dimensions of the mind as memory, self esteem, joy and creativity.

Concurrently, and almost antithetically, these same advances will facilitate the creation of molecules capable of altering brain functions in adverse fashion. New and overwhelmingly powerful hallucinogens and psychedelics will easily find their way into our knowledge base. These agents will have the capacity to metamorphose the sense of self, to alter belief systems and to favor the propensity to emit predetermined behaviors. Special caution in controlling their use will be imperative, lest they be employed to malignant ends.

The discovery of the nervous system is much like that of our universe. The more we see, the more there is to see. Insight is an ever more varied and detailed neuronal cartography, a cumulating awareness of the phantasmal sophistication of our neural networks, and an appreciation of how the protein microchips in our neurons - our genetic cryptogram - dynamically undulates with every electrochemical wave within our nervous system. The science of creating neurons from cell cultures, adapting them to specialized tasks, and non-injuriously directing them to specific areas in the nervous system will counteract many neurological and psychiatric syndromes, as it will equally be applied to enhance fitness. In time, our ability to work with neuronal genes - replacing, inserting, deleting and modulating them - will give individuals the opportunity to permanently alter their mood states, their psychological abilities and the expression of their everyday comportments.

While established psychiatric conditions, known since antiquity, such as schizophrenia and manic depressive illness will find therapeutic solutions, because they are strongly biologically driven, many other mental disharmonies will need further exploration and definition. This derives from the fact that an increasing spectrum of psychiatric conditions are being identified. It is now appreciated, for example, that there exist numerous kinds of depressions, and many varieties of anxiety disorders. The same applies to all other psychiatric diagnoses. In addition, as societies become more diverse and variegated, and play a role as harbingers of novel stressors, new syndrome are literally in the process of being created. From the appearance of "pure" hysterical reactions in the 19th century to the emergence of eating and sleeping disorders in the last decades of the 20th century, the new millennium will spawn psychiatric syndromes never exhibited before.

It is interesting to note in this regard that even with the spectrum of psychiatric treatments available today, the prevalence of all psychiatric disorders (except for schizophrenia) is increasing - depression, phobias, anxiety, affective illness, drug addiction, suicide, and aggressive disorders - a disturbing trend. Is the pace of modern life outdistancing the assistance psychiatry can provide?

Psychotherapy, the science of self-discovery and personal change will not disappear. Instead, it will evolve rapidly to become more focused and efficient. Techniques developed by other disciplines will provide this noble science with innovative tools. The use of virtual reality and interactive technology will greatly assist individuals in finding consonance in themselves and within the milieu of their increasingly multifaceted social environment.

On a social scale, as our planet comes to develop increasing compassion towards humanity's psychiatric travails, concerted efforts will emerge to assist communities and populations in crisis. A global network capable of psychiatrically aiding all people confronted with wars, epidemics, and natural calamities will evolve naturally from pure necessity. The expertise of the new science of societal dynamics will be called upon to assist in the resolution of national strifes, and in our third millennium, amidst some initial international turbulence, we will see the establishment of a world body whose mission will draw upon humanity's new grasp of social science wisdom to prevent catastrophes.

The next - and doubtlessly not the last - great frontier of psychiatry concerns the mind itself. What factors make the special phenomenon of experiencing thought and emotion an experience and not a robotic event? Although influenced by biochemical events, does being aware of one's own awareness make for a separate and distinct attribute of the mind? Does mind, as a miracle in its own right, belong to dimensions which, in spite of all our scientific sophistication, have still deftly eluded our scientific grasp? The spirit of the mind, much like the nature of our cosmology remains one of the most incandescent scientific questions in which the coming centuries will hopefully bestow their generous enlightenment.

In our lifetime, we will see astounding transformations affecting our environments, our bodies, and our minds. The conceptual caravans of the last millennia are giving way to rocket crafts. The possibilities of psychiatric sciences will pulverize our imagination as the secrets of the mind are extracted from the labyrinths of its bodily connections. In order to keep pace gracefully with the great changes that are to come, we will need to create innovative life philosophies and quantum vaults in our spiritual perspectives.

Reflections on Gerard V. Sunnen, M.D.

I have known Dr. Sunnen since he was a young man. I first met him when he accompanied his father to visit me. The discussion that day was their interest in the beneficial aspects of "hypnotic" techniques. Since that day, Dr. Sunnen and I have become good friends. He has attended many concerts of mine and written some beautiful reflections about my activities. It has given me a great source of satisfaction to have had some influence in the direction his life has taken. His background is simply incredible. He is a diplomat of the American Board of Psychiatry and Neurology, an Associate Clinical Professor of Psychiatry at New York University, the founder and Honorary President of the International Association for Emergency Psychiatry, as well as a member of two international clinical hypnosis organizations.

I have incorporated into this book the extensive commentary of Dr. Sunnen because I find his projections on psychiatry to be fascinating. I have said many times that I possess a lack of enthusiasm for psychiatrists, but Dr. Sunnen is one eminent exception. I value his opinions and his views.

His projections, and in some manner, his warnings, are based on how our view of the outer world has changed, and how psychiatry has expanded with it. His remarks describe neuro-chemical events in the brain and the role of neuron genes on our mental moods. His comments go on to talk about the great question of the relationship between the mind and the actual physical matter of the nervous system. Sunnen points out that Freud has stated that one day every thought would be physically traced in the brain at the moment of its occurrence. Dr. Sunnen tells us that the time has come.

Additionally, Dr. Sunnen points out that drugs and chemicals are going to become an important weapon in the treatment of serious psychiatric ills. This would be a drastic advance, as these ills have not responded to psychotherapies or condition reflex approaches to treatment. Chemicals, powerful and overwhelming, will find their way into our knowledge base as methods in altering not only behavior, but in altering belief systems. This is almost terrifying. What would happen if this technology came into the hands of the ruthless, the evil or the paranoid dictators of the world?

I find very intriguing Dr. Sunnen's comment that certain psychiatric disorders are increasing in our society - namely depression, phobias, anxieties, drug addiction, suicide, and aggressive disorders. He rightfully considers this a disturbing trend.

What I find most awesome in the comments of Dr. Sunnen is the concept that a global network will have the capacity to psychiatrically treat people confronted with wars, epidemics and natural calamities. This is what we have read about in science fiction over the past five decades. Does this also suggest mass healing, techniques of mass tranquillity? Or does it suggest techniques of mass control and influence?

Finally, I note that I have known Dr. Sunnen to be more than just a psychiatrist, but a philosopher as well. He speculates on the unique quality that we have within us - the ability to think about what we are thinking. No other being seems to have this ability. I discussed this in my first book, the 1960 release "The Amazing World of Kreskin." I suggested that it must be frustrating for a psychologist to have to grapple with this. Sunnen speaks almost metaphysically about the miracle of the mind and how it has still alluded our scientific grasp. As he speaks of the spirit of the mind, I see how remarkably Dr. Sunnen shows himself not only for his great psychiatric skills, but also his spiritual nature. This raises him far beyond mere psychiatry. His remarks are to be reflected upon, for if they prove accurate it will be miraculous how they will change man.

WULF H. UTIAN, M.D., Ph.D. - Menopause Research

Before the end of the next millennium, all the unanswered questions about menopause will have been explained and simple solutions towards dealing with its effects will have been developed. The mechanism by which the number of eggs within the ovary divide and then cease to multiply will have been elucidated so that technically menopause might be delayed and the age of fertility enhanced. Social, ethical, religious and scientific issues regarding the advanced reproductive technologies and their application to women beyond menopause will have been dealt with, but controversy will still linger as to the ethics of some of these applications. With regard to the hormonal activity of the ovary, all the ovarian steroidal and non-steroidal hormonal messengers (ligands) will be identified, their pattern of genetic and non-genetic behavior explained, derivatives synthesized, and clinical applications well-defined. Thus, there will be tissue selective estrogens that can be targeted to enhancing, for example, bone, without affecting any other tissues. Similar tissue selective estrogens will be developed to prevent heart disease, Alzheimer's disease, several auto-immune diseases, osteoporosis, and urogenital problems. Moreover, the interrelationship between these substances and the mechanisms for aging will also be explained so that the aging process will be delayed.

Women will live well beyond 100 years of age and the menopause will probably occur at around the half way point. Menopause will therefore be regarded as an extremely positive moment in life representing the passage into maturity. The amazing myths of menopause of the late second millennium will be viewed with mild amusement and wonder.

Reflections on Wulf H. Utian, M.D., Ph.D.

Certainly, Dr. Utian's projections are exciting, and in some cases inspiring. The idea that current studies might give us the key to controlling the mechanism of aging is truly intriguing. Dr. Utian mentions that women will live well beyond one hundred years of age. Since women have always outlived men, unless men's aging is significantly increased as well it is interesting to speculate how many husbands the average woman would have in a lifetime. I will not attempt to guess, or to try and get a mental impression. Let's just leave it for the next millennium.

SEYMOUR FISH, DDS - Dentistry

It has been 49 years since I entered Dental School, and in that time I have lived through monumental changes in dentistry. These changes are paltry compared to what is in the offing for the next fifty years.

The number one dental ailment has had its beginnings with tooth decay. It is responsible for the need to fabricate fillings, the death of the dental pulp (root canal therapy) and sometimes the loss of teeth necessitating a bridge. In the next 50 years, dental decay will be completely eliminated! We already know most of the organisms that cause decay, and in the future we will be able to counteract them with medication or vaccines. We have already strengthened the tooth's resistance through the use of fluorides.

The second major dental problem, and the greatest cause of tooth loss among adults is periodontal disease. This is a more complex disease process, but it also will be eliminated with the use of drugs and vaccines. This will involve eliminating the offending organisms, enhancing the immune system, and improving oral cleanliness chemically.

The present use of metal in the mouth in the form of restorations, such as amalgam fillings (now on the decline), gold inlays and crowns, and semiprecious metal fused to porcelain will be a thing of the past. The new restorations will be computer designed combinations of porcelain and plastic. The present use of a rotary drill will completely be replaced by lasers. Lasers will be used to cut, reshape and strengthen teeth.

The field of orthodontia will be changed drastically in the next fifty years by identifying incongruities between the size of the jaws, and the size of the teeth. With gene engineering, these mismatches will be eliminated. The future role of the dentist in the next hundred years will be limited to mostly preventive dentistry.

Reflections on Dr. Fish, DDS

I have known Dr. Fish for almost four decades and during that time I have seen remarkable changes in the sophistication of dentistry. Most people, at one time in their lives, have experienced anxiety at going to the dentist. As kids, most of us dreaded it. I can remember scores of cartoons where someone tied a string to an aching tooth and the other end to a doorknob. Pain was synonymous with dentistry.

In the 1950's, there was a strange introduction into the world of dentistry called the "hypnodentist." This concept revolved around the theory that a dentist trained in "hypnosis" could use the technique to alleviate or ease the pain. At one point, hypnodentistry seemed like a panacea, but like the rest of the hypnosis industry, it fell drastically to the wayside. I came to know Dr. Fish when he was employing hypnotic techniques. I like to think that it was my influence that caused him to give up the hypnosis modality. Eventually, nearly everyone who took up hypnosis in dental work simply gave it up as impractical, unrealistic, time consuming and ineffective. I remember one dental student telling me that a "scientific hypnotist" came to his school and worked in the clinic for a full day trying to extol the virtues of hypnosis. He was unable to effect any result with any of the patients. As time went by, it became clear that hypnosis had no effect at all in dentistry. The process' very small successes resulted from the patient's distraction, reassurance and the ability of the patient to relax some of the pain caused by apprehension.

Today, pain is almost an archaic part of dental history. The art of dentistry has progressed so miraculously that discomfort is almost unfelt in the dental office.

What has stuck in my mind these last few months is the reflection by Dr. Fish that in a few decades, the dentist as we know her will be a thing of the past. If I read between the lines, it is Dr. Fish's opinion that there will be fewer and fewer dentists as the years progress.

I see no signs of this trend being true regarding lawyers!

ALAN M. MacROBERT - Astronomer

We are already beginning to understand the cause of the Big Bang. It apparently has its origin in a larger, underlying space-time that spawns many Big Bang universes (perhaps an infinite number). These other universes are disconnected from our own. The nature and origin of the underlying "sub space," and how different physical laws and fundamental constants are set within each universe, will form the frontier of cosmology and physics by 2100.

By the year 3000 the planets of millions of stars, to a distance of hundreds of light-years, will be catalogued and classified. Many different types of solar systems will be recognized, and the abundance or rarity of Earth-like planets will be well known. Some of them, perhaps many, will show chemical signs in their atmospheres of having at least microbial life.

There will be permanent settlements on the Moon, Mars, and asteroids. Travel to even the nearest stars will still be out of reach.

We will probably be listening in on radio or other transmissions from intelligent creatures elsewhere in the universe. The senders will probably be unaware of our existence. Their radio traffic may provide a wealth of knowledge, or it may remain incomprehensible despite occupying a good fraction of world science. The nearest such civilization will be no closer than a couple thousand light-years, ruling out any chance for direct contact. Alternatively, if we have found no such transmissions, we will have searched for them so thoroughly to know that radio-capable intelligent life is extremely rare.

Reflections on Alan M. MacRobert

I asked Alan M. MacRobert his thoughts on the Universe and our interaction with it in the coming years. He prefaced his response to me with, "What a great idea -- get other people to write a book for you! I wish I'd thought of it!"

His sense of humor is topped only by his fascinating presentation. It truly is extraordinary to contemplate that we will have permanent settlements on the Moon, Mars, and asteroids. At the same time, Alan suggests that travel to even the nearest stars will remain inaccessible even in the next one thousand years.

As a mentalist and thought reader, what intrigues me most are his comments that we will be listening to radio transmissions of intelligent creatures somewhere else in the universe, even though they may be quite unaware of our presence.

In the 1940's, a psychologist friend who worked in the intelligence community, explained to me that the government's concerns surrounding extraterrestrial s was not the proof of UFO's or the proof of intelligent life beyond our own, but in the impact that such proof would have on our civilization. The common consensus was that "civilized man" would panic if there was clear proof that other creatures existed of far superior intelligence than anyone on earth. Discussions centered around man's reaction. Would there be panic, irrational behavior, or even violent behavior as earth's inhabitants tried to settle with the idea that our species could never achieve the intelligence of this "higher culture."

All of us at one time or another have had an experience similar to lying down on a the grass at night, looking up at the stars and wondered how far the sky goes. The next question is typically what is on the other side if the sky does end. Man struggles with the concept of infinity. It is difficult for us to fathom. The same limitations in our mind surround the Big Bang theory. To say the

Big Bang theory started it all, raises the question as to what started the Big Bang. There had to be some intelligence, some systematic cohesive thought. I have always enjoyed listening to the "reasoning" of the personality who would not accept the concept that there is a higher grade of intelligence than man. They become skillful in raising a subtle mental barrier using the convenience of a Big Bang theory, or a magical plant, or a miracle atom to explain our existence. The truth is they haven't answered much of anything. Will we ever have a full answer? That prediction is easy: NO!

BERTHOLD E. SCHWARZ, M.D. - Para-Normal
Expert

The millennium -- strong and set apart from other measurements of time -- will usher in a diversity of research for the advancement of understanding psychical phenomena. Knowledge and major accomplishments will then aggregate largely from studies focused on the world's natural resource of distinguished, gifted psychics. The counter-productive stonewalling, disassociations, denials, and obfuscations of the professional debunkers will crumble. A NEW era of intensive investigation will commence where the laboratory and statistics will become partners and adjuncts in psi clinical research to share with humankind phenomenal breakthroughs in all scientific fields. Medicine, and specifically psychiatry, will discover that in psi phenomena and its variegated manifestations, they have a sleeping giant that is now waking and ready for new investigatory techniques. Novel diagnostic and healing methods with the currently practiced functional nuclear magnetic resonance imaging (MRI), positron emission tomography (PET) and various other sophisticated electrographical and biochemical analyses will be enlisted in surveying the brain and the body, when gifted paragnosts are in rapport and entranced -- people who can, with some measure of predictability, demonstrate telepathy, clairvoyance, telekinesis, levitation, apportation, teleportation, direct writing, spontaneous combustion, and/or perhaps even materialization. The search for measurable changes in gifted paragnosts/psychics will be collated per collateral changes in matter, be they other people, or objects such as magnets, batteries, photons, chemical molecular effects on film or magnetic tape, and so forth.

The future will become more accessible and required changes implemented before unanticipated disasters occur. This will open a virtually unexplored frontier of priceless intelligence and knowledge.

The studies of inner space of the brain and body will rival what has been learned in outer space and also be equally practical -- and applicable -- to humans in the study of subtle forms of communication. For example, telepathy in parent-child relationships and/or psychotherapeutic transactions will be augmented and inch forward in understanding. The role of telepathy as the "forgotten" language and its vital component in learning language, in memory, and, when transformed to the body, its telepathic extension to various physical parameters such as the telesomatic reactions, will be respected. The role of unconscious attitude and possible psychic communications, which influence favorably as well as destructively various pathological conditions, will receive meticulous attention. And, hopefully, instead of building more and more prisons to punish and supposedly rehabilitate persons, which does NOT seem to be resolving issues, the maximum harvest of human potential -- now damages and/or destroyed -- will occur and bring LIGHT to those who are injured and/or destructive.

The deeper meanings of rapport, empathy, sympathy, and intuition will be examined from numerous perspectives. A richness and maximum length life span will begin. In the biological frontier in our own backyard, and in the Solar System, and throughout the known Universe, new life forms and undiscovered species will be revealed. On our planet, management of the forests and oceans will become priceless as we learn how ALL life is interdependent and expresses intelligence, direction, and evolution.

Humans are determined explorers. With the millennium, in-depth knowledge will finally become available about the human body's immune system. Immune mechanisms that are operative in fire immunity, will be extrapolated to the study of burns and relative degrees of immunity in those conditions as well as the role of cellular/tissue responses in healing, stigmata, organ transplantations, and various dermatological conditions. The presumed bio-chemical/electrical mediation of healing effects by recondite psychic factors will receive critical attention and, from this, major discoveries will be made regarding the role of these possible influences in the pathogenesis of disease states, e.g. the role of various hormones and biochemical mediators, and the isolation and development of new roles for neuro-transmitters, as well as the detecting of transmitters previously not thought of, and their interactions with various known drugs and chemicals. These discoveries will be enhanced by the already utilized bioinformatics techniques prevalent in the biotechnology industries and academe.

The now unraveling human gnome will also be prolifically applied to the gifted psychic and their families in the quest for common biological markets and factors of transmittal, as well as the specifics for the various forms of psi, e.g. telekinesis, levitation, apportation. These data will be coupled with well-established and refined techniques that fathom the psychology of these individuals and their unconscious mind. New ways to determine just what "suggestibility" (and various degrees of hypnosis) is and how it operates, in conjunction with psi in gifted persons -arguably society's MOST PRECIOUS ASSET and the new elite -- will be explored.

Statistics in 1998 show that one out of four people suffer mental health problems sometime in their life. Mental health, the robe and skull-cap of one's personality, is given an impolite gesture of dismissal now, towering as a character weakness. In the millennium, the psychiatrist will be able to analyze from another perspective the role of psi in dissociative disorders, in multiple personality, and in schizophrenic reactions. The role of unconsciously and telepathically transmitted thoughts and feelings that in the early parent-child relationship set the "mold" and/or are extremely influential in shaping the developing conscience for "good" character -- or lack of it (superego lacunae, in sociopathic disorders) -- will be probed and discoveries will be made. Such illnesses will be better understood and their treatments expedited. Learning and knowledge will surround every change.

Family structures will be reclaimed and researches into family dynamics incorporating psychic knowledge will be applied. Family structures that are aware and permissive and nurturing for psi potential in children can yield a harvest of paragnosts who by their gifts and accomplishments can expand knowledge that will benefit everyone. Trying to grind psi and its resulting physical, mental, and sometimes spiritual phenomenon under the heel of one's boot, forbidding its expression, only sidetracks the gifted paragnost(s) into diverse forms of psychopathology. Perhaps ways of measuring psi itself -- rather than indirect studies on its effects on the psychic and/or the consultants -- can be incorporated. The actual measurement, calibration, and definition of the psi "energy" which does NOT seem to conform to the electromagnetic spectrum will yield clues of the most amazing and refractive of its forms: precognition. This will, as well, leave its mark on many aspects of accepted science and currently developing theories of the mind.

What sets those gifted psychic individuals apart from those who do NOT have this faculty? How does it tie in with other related psi abilities? Why, for example, does telekinesis and precognition -- when stressed or activated -- flare, rather than demonstrate a psychosomatic reaction (asthma attack) or forms of acting out (delinquency)? What emergency neural and body mechanisms are triggered when, for example, a person is suddenly able to demonstrate remarkable strength, to lift an excessively heavy object like a car or slab of pig iron? Or looking at psi historically, could psi have been a factor in the moving of heavy blocks of granite or stone in construction of the pyramids and sacred temples? Could psi apportation account for Fortean artifacts or foreign bodies, e.g. a necklace found in the bottom of a coal mine? Or various UFO artifacts, such as claimed but poorly documented "implants"?

Other millennial crops ripe for harvesting are the modern extrapolations of the earlier, classical psychic feats as illustrated in automatic and/or direct writing of numerous texts noted through the years, and which would be otherwise unaccountable: Oaspe, Urantia, Patience Worth, and Bridey Murphy. Specifically, clues for pursuing psi might also be found in the renaissance of human/computer interactions where these mechanisms now in 1999 defy knowledge of electronics where, for example, the computer activates (the monitor screen lights and then has messages) when the electrical current is NOT physically connected. Where does this knowledge (or messages) come from? How can one predict with precision what will follow after the communication(s) happen? And in some instances, what about the timing of these messages? All of the above have happened to people, seemingly at times independent of the person's conscious inclinations and knowledge.

There is so much to accomplish and now more than ever is the need for explorers to venture into the unknown. How great the debt of gratitude is to all those who have left their marks in this heroic quest through the past millennium, particularly from the ancient shamans, prophets, and sorcerers, to the modern and gifted paragnosts who have often withstood ridicule and derision, if not burning at the stake for standing Herculean and strong with their impressions. I specifically honor the many unsung and unnamed who have helped my investigations and also the superparagnosts whom I was privileged to know and study: Jacques Romano, Joseph Dunninger, and Gerard Croiset. Today the chief luminary on the scene is my friend Kreskin who with his telepathic skills brings warmth and delight to millions of people with entertaining and thought provoking showmanship. From the spontaneity, fun, awe, and levity of his public demonstrations much can be learned -- and on a deep, serious level, Kreskin is an example of unique talent that has too often been ignored by major research in academe, distinguished institutions, and think tanks. This <u>will</u> change in the millennium.

We look forward to a great adventure -- a voyage into the unknown.

Reflections on Berthold E. Schwarz, MD

I have known Psychiatrist Dr. Berthold Schwarz for years and find him to be one of the most dynamic and electrifying people one could ever meet. He is an encyclopedia of knowledge in the fields of psychiatry and psychotherapy, as well as the extrasensory perception and para-normal phenomena. You can ask him about almost any topic regarding the para-normal and he can quote you passage and verse studies and findings on the subject. Dr. Schwarz either knows personally or is close communication with virtually any authority on the subject that has worked in the field in the past fifty years.

In general, I have never been a big fan of psychiatrists. I find them to be, as a group, the most mentally troubled in our society. However Dr. Schwarz in an exception. He is a brilliant man. Being in his presence is almost therapeutic, as he has an incredible zest for life. He has an innate cheerfulness, a way of looking at any situation, no matter how stressful, and finding some positive flavor or spark. If all of the investigators in the field of the para-normal possessed his spirited enthusiasm, I believe that more people would take the area of extrasensory perception seriously. His credentials are impeccable and inspiring. He has a very successful private practice and has served as a fellow in psychiatry at the Mayo Foundation.

His investigations of telepathic communications truly intrigue me. He has worked extensively on telepathy between parents and their children, as well as physicians and their patients. Sigmund Freud hinted at the concept of doctor/patient telepathy, but he did not attempt to push it extensively for fear of losing followers of his theory of psychoanalysis.

In recent years, I have come to the conclusion that anyone who is frustrated with life, or in need of attention, can become a debunker of the para-normal. I see this often with second rate magicians. I say this not to denigrate magicians in general, but the profession of conjuring has been seriously shortchanging para-normal phenomena. If the skeptics took a moment to look back on history, they would see that the majority of truly great magicians, from Houdini to Keller to Thurston, believed in certain areas of para-normal phenomena -- like telepathy, precognition and clairvoyance. Skeptics today seem more interested in perpetuating a negative image on the field, than on searching for the truth. The narrow rules and conditions that have been established by the skeptics for testing ESP ensure the failure of the tests. If the same rules and conditions were used in testing the field of psychology, that too would be a rapidly debunked science. 1, for one, am not sure that psychology deserves the classification as a science. However, psychologists are reluctant to give any credence to ESP or to take on any issue that is controversial for fear that the spotlight will be turned on their own work. And the tests would fail.

While we might not all agree with all of the convictions of Dr. Schwarz, he must be admired and respected for his courage to traverse an area that is so controversial. The majority of psychologists, psychiatrists and philosophers immediately strip all perceived credibility from anyone who hints at the possibility that there is some truth to para-normal phenomena. Dr. Schwarz is brave enough to stand up and speak of his beliefs.

As for the skeptics intended effect on the public, they seem to be losing. The popularity in recent years of metaphysical subjects and television shows dealing with the unknown attest to the fact that skeptics are actually having the opposite effect than they had hoped for. Instead of brainwashing the public into scoffing at the para-normal, they have increased interest. While the skeptics drone on that ESP does not exist, the public, and many professionals, know better and realize that there is something that the investigators are missing. Dr. Schwarz's writings the contemporary interests and curiosities of today's society.

A few months back, I sat with some two hundred students at a university, watching a network presentation on belief. The show turned out to be focused on debunking various fringe para-normal claims and personalities. About halfway through the hour-long program, there were less than a eighteen students remaining. I consider myself a good listener -- I can usually hear a low whisper from across the room. As students left the room, I could here them speaking to each other and saying that this program was just a rehash of the same old material. The same skeptical comments were being broadcast again. The students were more than bored, they craved new information. They didn't believe the skeptics and wanted a new perspective, new information. The students' reaction was remarkable and it showed that once again the communication media has lost touch with their audience.

When you have a moment, choose a few paragraphs from Dr. Schwarz's commentary and reflect upon it. He has some exciting thoughts that could find their way into the new millennium.

DAVID SATCHER, M.D., Ph.D. - Assistant
Secretary For Surgeon General

Dear Mr. Kreskin: Thank you for your letter in which you requested my thoughts on how disease control will change in the next 1,000 years.

As Assistant Secretary for Health and Surgeon General, I am a public official subject to the Standards of Ethical Conduct issued by the U.S. Office of Government Ethics. Under those standards and implementing requirements of the Department of Health and Human Services, I must refrain from any action that would give preferential treatment to a private organization or individual, or give the appearance of doing so. As you might expect, I receive numerous requests to endorse of otherwise support individuals, private publications, funding applications, new products, and the like. In order to avoid any question of favoritism under the Standards of Conduct, it is my practice not to endorse or support such activities. There might be an occasion where, for important health reasons, I might do so, but that would occur only very rarely and where there would be important Federal public health justifications involved.

For the foregoing reasons, I must decline your request to provide input for inclusion in the book you are developing.

Reflections on David Satcher, M.D., Ph.D.

There is little more I can add to the comments of Dr. Satcher. Knowing that he is a public official that is subject to the standards and ethics issued by the government, we have to be impressed by his reason for declining from an activity that might be interpreted as preferential treatment. Can you imagine if Members of Congress exercised the same restraint and caution? I am not sure that such a standard could ever be maintained when you consider the make-up of the people who control our Congress.

On the other side of the coin, it is a shame from an educational viewpoint the Dr. Satcher did not take the opportunity to educate us as to what we might expect in the area of disease control in the next 1,000 years. I think that would have been an important service to the American public, but we must respect his concern for the standards of conduct.

ALAN CARUBA - National Anxiety Center

The greatest change for Americans will be who we are within a century or so after the Millennium arrives. Americans will increasingly be Hispanic and Asian. Caucasians, the dominant racial group throughout the past two centuries, will become a minority. There will be considerable intermarriage between members of all of these groups, including Afro-Americans, creating a unique, racially mixed American citizen unlike any other nation in the world. In the new Millennium, Americans will have to cope with the middle-eastern movement of Muslims whose faith teaches them that everyone will ultimately accept Islam. When this does not occur, either Islam will adapt itself to a new age or the struggles between Islamic sects will metastasize into major ruptures.

American Jews and those Jews remaining worldwide will diminish greatly by as early as 2001. Inter-marriage and assimilation will lessen their already small numbers.

The next Millennium bodes well for democracy and a global marketplace, but not without a struggle with ancient forces still favoring socialism, despotism, and dictatorship. Two American driven factors will triumph, however. The inevitable spread of media and Internet communications will spread democratic concepts worldwide. The other factor will be the appeal of American culture and American ideals.

In the coming Millennium, Americans will see an explosion of small nation-states emerge from within Russia and China, and on the African continent as well.

Despite its announced intention to impose a global government, the United Nations, like any vast bureaucracy, will ultimately implode, judged incapable of dealing with rapidly changing events.

The good news is that people all over the world will live longer, healthier lives, with plenty of food and energy resources. The world's population will ultimately stabilize, decreasing as greater prosperity is shared by everyone.

Reflections on Alan Caruba

I have severe difficulties with some of the remarks of Mr. Caruba. However, Mr. Caruba, a 61 year old veteran business and science writer, has a remarkable and panoramic view of the social structure of society. One cannot doubt for a moment his suggestion that the Hispanic and Asian proportions in our society will increase. We see signs of this trend already. His prediction that there will be considerable intermarriage amongst all racial groups is interesting, and is how it should be. If we honestly listen to our theologians and philosophers we must agree that man is created equal, and that the color or the shape of the eyes has nothing to do with the quality of the man. Caruba also remarks that the Muslim faith teaches the ultimate acceptance of Islam. This is not the only religious philosophy that suggests the eventually of all man accepting such beliefs. To suggest that it could evolve into major ruptures is certainly something to be concerned about, but is not limited to the Muslim faith. In fact, that theory would incorporate most of the World's religions.

I must admit that the suggestion Caruba makes that the number of Jews will diminish as early as 2001 is clearly inaccurate. I can't even remotely believe that such will be the case. Caruba may speak of small numbers, but he fails to speak of the strength and conviction of the Jewish culture. If anything, I have a strong feeling that the Jewish movement will become stronger in the years to come as the World shows its respect for a people that own one of the longest legacies of any group still in existence on the face of the earth.

Caruba's comment that we will see an explosion of small nation states emerging within Russia and China is intriguing. We may already be seeing this trend in Russia. Exactly how it might happen in China is open to a great deal of conjecture.

I also find interesting Caruba's prediction that the United Nations will collapse. I agree that he is correct on the subject. The question is what organization will take its place, and will the new organization be capable of accomplishing what the United Nations couldn't.

It is refreshing that Caruba ended on a favorable note, that man will live longer and healthier lives. At first, I was taken aback by the prediction there will be plenty of food and energy resources. This is surprising when in parts of the United States there may already be signs that water is not easily accessible. Perhaps Caruba sees the food and energy prediction as a byproduct of his prediction that the world population will stabilize. It is clear that if the population continues to explode upward, the downfall of society could result. There are only so many resources on this earth.

WARREN ECKSTEIN - Pet Therapist

As we enter the new Millennium, I hope that man will realize the importance of all the living creatures we are blessed to coexist with.

By creating a broader awareness of the human-animal bond through animal-assisted therapy, we continue to expand the role of the animal. Animal-assisted therapy unites certified animals and their volunteer handlers in the therapy of physically, cognitive, psychological and physiologically challenged individuals. In settings as diverse as Veteran Rehabilitation to Autistic programs, the therapeutic advantage of animals, from Golden Retrievers to Dolphins, is astounding.

If we, as human beings, can only learn the respect the animal kingdom possesses for each other, then there would never be another endangered species, because it is man who creates extinction. I choose to devote my life to the animals because of their honesty and ability to forgive. It is my silent prayer that future generations will preserve and safeguard this legacy, because a world without animals would truly not be a world worth living in.

Reflections on Warren Eckstein

I have never met a person more reflective of what life is all about than Warren Eckstein. If love is the powerful force that bridges man's communications, then Warren Eckstein has taken love a step farther by including our animal world.

I have known Warren Eckstein for over a decade and cannot help but admire his remarkable ability to communicate with animals. This ability sometimes reaches a telepathic level. In a bygone era, more open-minded psychologists believed that there was some type of mental communication between animals and their masters. (I am not sure that the word master is justifiable in the ideal relationship between pets and their human companions.) There are many cases on record showing animals finding their way back home after becoming separated from their families. Sometimes the distances the pet traveled extended for hundreds of miles, over a number of states. Pets are gifted with an incredible degree of sensitivity, which may only find itself in man on rare occasions. If one has doubts as to the existence of telepathy, then look no farther for proof then pets. They know when their human companions are sad or happy, and in spite of human tendencies towards uncertain behavior, they are loyal. Animals simply do not betray people. Warren Eckstein both practices and preaches the ideal treatment that animals so richly deserve. I don't believe Warren could pass a lonely or lost animal on the street without stopping and helping out. Do yourself a favor and find one of the books he wrote, titled, "Memoirs of a Pet Therapist." If your reaction is like mine, you'll be in tears as you read about his incredible love for the animal world.

Throughout my life I have owned many animals, including chickens, rabbits, dogs, and cats. Currently I have three cats, named Miss Kitty, ET, and Squeaky. I chose cats because of my intense travel schedule. They can take good care of themselves, and while I do have people around to care for them, they also make good companions for each other. When I return home from a trip, they all gather around me welcoming me back into the fold. I am told that when I am away that they show signs of missing me, their behavior alters somewhat. The bond between animals and their human companions is obvious. Whenever he comes across any animal, Eckstein will simply approach it and kiss it. The animal clearly senses the love. Human/animal interaction is fascinating. I have had the opportunity to sit down and talk with Siegfried and Roy, the great Las Vegas illusionists. They have a passionate love for animals that is clearly returned. They work with Bengal tigers and other rare exotic cats that usually can only be found in zoos or remote jungle areas. Siegfried and Roy's caring and love for their animals creates a bond that the cats respond to, and the mutual respect and admiration makes the entire show a success. One thing is for sure, if you want to gain insight into a particular person, observe how they treat animals and you will learn an awful lot.

As for Warren's comments, I found his remark that animal assisted therapy can be so important to challenged individuals very thought provoking. I remember a few years ago when some retirement homes began a program where they brought pets into the wards of patients who had begun to feel forgotten. The program was a huge success and has been spreading throughout the country. Introducing animals as a therapeutic addition to the rehabilitation and convalescence of individuals is to me a remarkable step in therapy. Warren Eckstein is clearly the pioneer in this movement.

DR. PAUL KURTZ - Professor of Philosophy

It is difficult to predict the future with precision, for the contingent and unexpected are pervasive features of the human adventure. There are, however, various scenarios that we can project into the future. I think that the doomsday prophecies are exaggerated. I prefer to emphasize the promising opportunities that are available to humankind, given the fact that 90% of all scientists that have ever lived are now alive. I think that science and technology will continue to surprise and excite us with new discoveries.

Medical and biogenetic research will conquer many diseases and extend life considerably. Living standards will improve worldwide. With rising levels of influence, population growth will be restrained. New sources of energy will be discovered. Education and literacy will increase enormously and people will be able to pursue more significant and rewarding lives. Space travel will become commonplace. In a time, a new global ethics will develop. All of this depends on the development of appreciation of both scientific methods of inquiry and shared humanistic values. The Human Prospect, barring some unforeseen catastrophe, may be viewed in glowing, affirmative, and optimistic terms!

Reflections on Dr. Paul Kurtz

Dr. Kurtz is a renowned Professor of Philosophy at the State University of New York at Buffalo. He has been active in the American Humanist movement and is editor in chief of Free Inquiry. He is also founder and chairman of the Committee for the Scientific Investigation of Claims of the Paranormal. That organization is bent on discrediting anything dealing with the paranormal, the supernatural, metaphysical, and areas of religious miracles. If you pick up any of their books authored by the organization's officers you will find they have a consistent secular way of finding no evidence of paranormal phenomena. Indeed, there is no doubt in my mind that if someone walked in the middle of the Atlantic Ocean the members would spend the next thirty-seven years looking for wires under the surface of the sea.

I appeared at one of their national conventions to speak about the myth of hypnosis. During a panel discussion the audience seemed receptive to my points, designed to show the lack of existence of any hypnotic state at all. I began to feel that the audience had the character of a religious revival meeting. They all had a mind set of "not believing" and neither I nor they were entirely sure of what it was they didn't believe in. Identifying this audience's mind set, I concluded that if a person believes in all areas of paranormal phenomena, then it is almost impossible for him to see the illegitimate or fraudulent phenomena, so blind would their belief be. I saw hundred of faces nodding in agreement, but I hadn't finished my sentence. I added that those who do not believe in any form of paranormal phenomena will find it most difficult to accept even legitimate proof! I saw the magicians, psychologists, philosophers and scientists in the audience sit for a stunned moment. I treasure that moment.

Incidentally, an affiliate of the Committee for the Scientific Investigation of Claims of the Paranormal, Prometheus Publications, republished one of my books under the title, "Secrets of the Amazing Kreskin." The book is still offered by their company. It was only after the release of the book that I discovered that one word had been edited from my own writings -- it was on the last page, and it was a reference to God.

I must admit to being tremendously delighted with Dr. Kutz's reflections. In many ways, it is much more positive and expresses much more optimism than many of today's religious leaders who have speculated on the future. It is refreshing to find that he considers the doom and gloom to be exaggerated. Like the more positive philosophers of the 30's and 40's, he looks upon the years to come with optimistic vision. Some of us would well to read his entry three or four times -- I certainly have.

COTE & HALL - National Fire Protection Assoc.

The millennium just ending had only two centuries of what we think of as technology, after the Industrial Revolution, and only about one century of technology applied to fire safety. Yet in that one century, we have been able to reduce the chances of dying in a fire and the amount of our annual income lost to fire by a factor of six. What miracles of fire safety might we achieve with another thousand years to work? In the next millennium, people will be surrounded with safety sensors -- the sophisticated descendants of today's smoke alarms. Sampling temperature, particles, gases, and more, these sensors will quickly detect fires, gas leaks, and other emergencies, and trigger responses from other built-in systems, the descendants of today's fire sprinklers.

The next millennium's fire suppression systems will have an agent application point close by any potential fire source and will have a range of agents designed for any kind of fire. But these emergency sensors and suppressors will have far fewer fires to address because of other changes. Sensors built into our equipment will detect overheats, gas leaks, short circuits and other hazardous conditions before they can cause an emergency situation. This "smart" equipment, used throughout our new "smart" houses and buildings, will stop problems before they start.

The materials that once provided the first fuels or the worst fuels in fires will change as new generations of materials -- designed at the molecular level to achieve specific fire performance objectives as well as other functions -- will resist ignition better and burn slower, less fiercely, and with fewer, milder, byproducts.

Finally, our descendants in the next millennium will be much smarter -- including fire safety smarter -- in using all this wondrous new "stuff." Knowledge of fire science and fire safety will be provided early to children and reinforced effectively through lifelong learning. Junior High school students will understand fire as well as today's college-educated specialty engineers, and their much younger siblings will understand fire safety as well as the most -fire-conscious adult does today. Some of these wonders will happen in our lifetimes.

The future of fire safety is a real future -- but it will seem like magic.

Reflections on Cote & Hall

Arthur E. Cote and Dr. John R. Hall, Jr. are prominent figures in the National Fire Protection Association, and their reflections are certainly most reassuring. During my childhood, I had an uncle who, in addition to his full time job, became the volunteer fire chief in my hometown. Since then, I have been aware of the potential, devastating dangers of fire. From seeing fires being fought by courageous firemen or from seeing the reflection of evil in the fires from the burning of Atlanta in Gone With The Wind, we all are aware of the very real terror fire can create. Having lived through an earthquake in Los Angeles, I can assure you that the first thing that enters your mind after the shaking stops and you regain your senses, is whether there are any fires breaking out nearby. The comment about sensors of the future being able to quickly detect not only fires, but gas leaks and other potential emergency situations is reassuring. This high degree of sensitivity and alertness causes me to reflect upon the technique involved in my telepathic demonstrations. It is almost as if the fire protection techniques are extra-sensory. As Cote and Hall said at the end, it certainly does "seem like magic!"

SALLY E. SMITH - Fat Acceptance, Inc.

The new millennium will transform the community of fat people. In 1998, the National Institute of Health redefined obesity as to affect at least 25 million more Americans. By these standards, the obese comprise a startling 55% of the population. Yet even though fat people are in the majority, the discrimination and social stigma against large Americans runs rampant. They are discriminated against in employment, education, in access to public accommodations, and in access to adequate medical care. They are fair game for everyone from comedians to passersby on the street.

In the new millennium, fat people may reject the notion that size is a character flaw. They will reject the premise of a multi-billion dollar weight loss industry that permanent weight loss is possible. They will reject the notion that second-class treatment is all they deserve. Instead, the future will see people of all sizes of large stop obsessing about thinness and instead work toward political and social change.

We may see legislation enacted that would give an avenue of redress to the victims of size discrimination. We may see airlines actually sell passage for one person, instead of demanding that fat people buy two seats. We may see fat people demanding unbiased care from their health professionals. We may see movie theaters, restaurants, and other public places have seating to accommodate our larger citizens. We may see size issues added to other diversity programs in schools, so fat kids will no longer commit suicide when they can no longer take the taunts of their classmates.

In the process, we may educate the 45% of the population that is of average size, so that everyone understands that beauty, intelligence and compassion comes in all shapes and sizes.

Reflections on Sally E. Smith

Ms. Smith is the Executive Director of the National Association to Advance Fat Acceptance, Inc. I got a kick out of the memo she sent to me along with her predictions. It read, "I would be **happy to expand** the piece if you are interested." I share this thought meaning the gentlest of humor, as I can identify with her cause. Many of my closest friends and relatives would have, in the past, been described as "fat people." I never saw them as such. Their humor, love and hugability made them special people throughout my life. I agree with Ms. Smith that fat people have been, at times, discriminated against. On the flip side, however, fat people have engendered a special kind of rapport in both entertainment and private life. There are many places in the world, such as the former Soviet Union where weight has been considered a positive quality. Beauty is in the eye of the beholder and I know many people who are both beautiful and fat.

Miscellaneous

ALAN GREENSPAN - Chairman of The Federal Reserve Bank

We ran into Mr. Greenspan at the Architect of Peace Awards at the Century Plaza Hotel in Los Angeles and were able to ask him a number of questions regarding his predictions for the economy.

Q: Do you see any major economic trends coming in the new millenium?

A: I believe the economy will continue to be robust, if that is what you are asking.

Q: Are there any emerging trends?

A: The World is becoming much more global, and the economy of one country is becoming increasingly reliant, and effected by, the economy of other countries.

Greenspan's predictions centered on his feeling that the economies of various nations are becoming interdependent. While he predicted that the US economy would "continue to be robust" he pointed out the increasingly difficult job of keeping the economies of major nations strong. A weakening economy in a major nation would affect others.

Reflections on Alan Greenspan

Alan Greenspan is the head of the Federal Reserve Bank. The stock market is directly and dramatically affected by any comments Mr. Greenspan makes, as he is the one that sets interest rates. No one has more impact on the United States economy than Alan Greenspan. It is also easily argued that no one has more impact on the World's economy than Alan Greenspan. As the head of the Federal Reserve Bank, it is Greenspan's job to keep the U.S. economy booming. One of his primary tools in this endeavor is his power to set interest rates. Greenspan gives economy status updates to Congress and the World holds its collective breath when he talks. If he hints interest rates will be lowered to slow inflation, the Stock Market booms, if he gives the impression he might raise interest rates to slow down an economy moving too fast, the market drops. His power is tangible and immense.

WOLFGANG PUCK -- Chef to the Stars

Wolfgang Puck is one of the most famous chefs working today. His restaurants play host to many of today's hottest celebrities. He is the guest on many talk shows and caters many of Hollywood biggest events. He became famous as the owner and chef at the Beverly Hills restaurant Spago. He now owns many restaurants from the upscale Spago to the cookie-cutter pizza restaurants in airports.

Q: Do you see any trends emerging for the new millenium?

A: How so?

Q: Types of restaurants people will enjoy, types of food?

A: People love quality dining, that will always be.

Q: If you were building a restaurant for the next millenium, what would you do to ensure success.

A: Excellent food, and a dining experience. People like to enjoy the meal and the surroundings, atmosphere.

Reflections on Wolfgang Puck

As a performer who has traveled the world, I can predict that the public will expect more from their restaurant than simply excellent food. The restaurant customer of the future will expect a dining experience that fosters human communication. In the future, the dining experience will not include loud, blasting noise and taped music. The public will grasp for opportunities to relate with each other. As the computer narrows one's lifestyle, keeping people in their homes more, dining out will become a special experience. Consequently, people will at long last look for a chance to hear each other while they are eating. There is little question that noise has a stressful effect on a person, and it is certainly not a good idea to digest food when the nervous system is tense. There are restaurants today that are so loud, due to no carpeting, no drapes, or simply blaring music, that at times it is simply impossible to hear the person you are dining with. There will be a day when we learn from the Europeans that eating is a special experience. We will also learn that noise and candlelight are contradictions.

We can save the noise for the fast food restaurants where the customer is already tense and the noise simply reinforces his high stress lifestyle. However, I predict that in the years to come, the public will demand to be able to enjoy the taste of their food by savoring not only its smell and flavor, but the sound surrounding it. That would the recipe for an extraordinarily successful restaurant.

ARTHUR FRIEDMAN - Fashion

The best way to project what fashion might look like in the next millennium is to see how it evolved over the last 1,000 years.

Of course, for most of that time, fashion was confined to basic needs, such as keeping people warm and covering what wasn't to be seen. People basically made clothes from vegetable fibers woven into garments or from metallic coverings used for battle. Clothes were handmade, either by women at home sewing for their family or by tailors and craftsmen sewing for the elite of society.

The last 100 years gives us more tangible evidence of what is to come. The invention of the sewing machine and the advent of a merchant economy gave rise to a variety of dressing styles and an avenue for entrepreneurs to creatively influence the way people dress. Paris and New York became the design Meccas of the world, places where the creations and marketing of apparel lines dressed the masses and upper echelon of the globe.

In the last 25 years, brands and labels became almost as important as the trends themselves. From Nike and Reebok to Hugo Boss and Georgio Armani, the image of the brands has become status symbols of what is hip and cool. Brands also played into the consumer need to feel comfortable with their purchase. Trusting a brand's integrity makes it easier to shop -- just buy whatever your favorite store and brand is showing that season.

Going into the next century, the Internet Revolution is and will continue to dramatically change the way people shop for fashion. Virtual stores are already seeing exponential growth in online sales, and it's just the beginning. The ability to buy what you want anytime of day or night at the click of a mouse is fast becoming what will soon be a mainstream way of doing business.

Now, some of these big brands and stores are joining in on the bandwagon to ensure their survival. They've also changed their stores and malls into entertainment vehicles replete with amusement parks and climbing walls, coffee shops and food courts -- all to attract customers.

How fashion will change in the future seems totally dependent on technology. With advanced computers, people will undoubtedly be able to holographically see the latest look and be fitted like the best couturier. They'll be able to shop online together with their friends on virtual trips to the mall. They'll be able to imagine how they look in a particular outfit by software packages that scan the user's body and show it on screen.

Looking ahead 1,000 years, fabrics will someday be so comfortable and weather resistant that they will sustain the extremes of cool and hot on hearth, the moon, mars and other planets yet to be discovered. Clothing for space or underwater living will need to be resilient beyond today's imagination, but as the human race evolves intellectually, what you wear will not be as important as what you need to wear to accomplish your life's mission. There are signs of this change already occurring, as offices and restaurants ease dress codes to conform to a society that increasingly doesn't care about being dressy as much as it does about being comfortable.

It's impossible to guess what people will be wearing in the year 3000, but I'm sure people from the year 1000 would be in shock if they saw the latest looks from the runways or walked into the Mall of America or the newest Niketown.

Reflections on Arthur Friedman

The remarks of Arthur Friedman, Associate Editor of Woman's Wear Daily, are intriguing and illuminating. He points out that clothing began as a tool for warmth and covering, and has evolved to a reflection of one's life style. This evolution makes the study of clothing part of the study of mankind. Society, individuality, and technology are all seen in clothing trends.

Friedman also speaks of the Internet revolution. He predicts the Internet will change the way people shop for fashion. They will be able to make purchases any time of day or night, with the mere click of a mouse.

I find fascinating his prediction that man will be able to look at holographic forms and see the latest look. The ability to be fitted by the couturier and the results projected on our computer screen is exciting. The one area of holographic shopping Mr. Friedman didn't mention is the ability to "feel" how comfortable the texture of the clothing will be when we actually wear it. I predict this addition will be part of the entire transaction.

CASEY BUSH - Headwear Information Bureau

As we enter the new millennium, fashion will continue to take the liberty of defining who we are and who we are not. With personal preferences taking such divergent paths from a social and professional level, most people won't have the time to indulge in all fashion trends, all the time.

With this in mind, to roll the camera ahead a few hundred years, we will see a melding of fashion tastes, leaving little to the imagination for daytime wear. There will be no time for extraneous fashion decisions. Everyone will be busy with time travel, e-mail, interplanetary relationships, video mail, virtual reality seminars, internal reality checks, and memory consorting. Therefore, daytime fashions will give us uniformity and simplicity: a one-piece slip on suit for no nonsense dressing. To express individuality, HATS and accessories will be mandatory. The Hat will define your mood and social status. The casual daytime hat will play a vital role as a protector from the elements. The hat will shield you from ultra-violet sun rays and the "40% body heat loss through the top of the head" shivers.

For evenings, the ornamented-decorated hat will take preference for style and excitement and will set you apart from the crowd. Hats will be a power magnet and a quick fix make-over with jewelry additions to change a look from office to opera. Of course, HEADWEAR will come in fabrics that don't wrinkle or fade. They can have shine and easily fit in your pocket.

No one will leave the house without a hat. A hat will embrace your lifestyle, your identity, and your better health.

Reflections on Casey Bush

Casey Bush's remarks on the new millennium are certainly "off the top of his head." The prediction that hats will return and play a more defining role in our daily lives is interesting. The concern about ultra-violet rays, coupled with the fact that most body heat is lost through the head, gives headwear a medicinal benefit. As a seasoned winter camper, I recognize that the hat has been the most singularly overlooked piece of clothing in recent years. Throughout history, hats have been very important. From the great picture show piece hats that were promenaded on a Ziegfield-like pathway on stage to the elegance of the country gentleman to the magician with his top hat, headwear has made all the difference in style. We have let so many years go by without acknowledging that a hat could tell us more about a person than his simple trade as a policeman or a pilot.

To me, the most interesting remark Bush makes is that the hat will become the most convenient expression of one's mood and social status in a world busy with time travel and interplanetary relationships. As I regress back to my early career as a magician, I think that in this entry "we really pulled something out of the hat!"

LARRY HELTON - educator

Most would say that the latest in technology will be employed in the schools of tomorrow. However, just as the Book or Revelation states the end battle will be on horseback, so will schools revert back to the ways of earlier times. Education will revert to the times when the 3 R's and the tune of the hickory switch were important in the educational process. With the "dumbing down of America" continuing to produce an undisciplined youth without the basic skills of reading, writing and arithmetic, schools will need to change their ways. The education system will be forced to spend less time with alternative learning and the use of gadgets and simply turn back to yesteryear. Teaching of the 3 R's and corporal punishment will once again be the norm in order to regain a productive society.

Reflections on Larry Helton

Mr. Helton offers a refreshing and, in many respects, positive outlook on the future of education. At a time when the United States' grade and high school education system is failing, it is clear that change will be inevitable. I find his prediction that corporal punishment will return as the norm to be interesting. He adds to that the rejection of alternate learning techniques and the end of learning gadgets. What is left is a return to the educational systems of yesteryear. Helton sees this return to the basic approach to teaching our children as the remedy to the tragic demise of the education quality in the U.S. His prediction that the "tune of the hickory switch" will return is not so shocking as it seems. We see an avalanche of evidence that teachers are becoming nothing more than guards, as teaching becomes secondary to controlling chaos in the classrooms.

It wasn't that long ago that if you misbehaved in class you were slapped and reprimanded by the teacher. If we are going to return to corporal punishment it might be wise to first slap the child for his behavior and follow that up with a slap to the parent!

PAT ROBERTSON - religious leader

Dear Mr. Kreskin

Thank you for your letter of September 1 5th with the request that I participate in the book you are writing.

In 1990 1 wrote a book, The New Millennium, which outlined 10 trends that will impact every individual and every family by the year 2000.

Beyond this, I really have no interest in participating in another book on the subject.

Sincerely, Pat Robertson Chairman of the Board, Chief Executive Officer, The Christian Broadcasting Network, Inc.

Reflections on Pat Robertson

I am including the response of Mr. Pat Robertson because I think it will enable some to gain a bit of insight into his personality. I did not realize he had written a book in 1990 with some kind of prophecy. I say it must have included some type of prophecy since he presumed in the book to outline what trends would impact society by the year 2000. 1 would have found it interesting if he had expounded on his views from the book, explaining whether his views had heightened or his predictions began to take shape in reality since he made them in 1990.

Another interesting area would be in the field of politics. Robertson ran for President because he said he had a calling from God to do so. With a new election coming up, it would have been interesting to hear his views on the political gathering of votes may alter in the years to come. At any rate, I think his last comment sums it up -- he really has no interest in participating in another such book, and I must respect him for such.

PHIL BLAZER - publisher, International Jewish News

With the close of the 1990's, World Jewry is apprehensive about its future due to the rise of intermarriage and the political and religious disunity in Israel.

The beginning of the new millennium will witness a new direction in approaching the inter-married couple by successfully formulating a campaign to attract the new family towards Judaism. Although the orthodox Jewish community has been against proselytizing since the Middle Ages, there will be a reversal of this position in order to combat a population decrease. Positioning Judaism as a religion of the individual void of guilt and salvation, a growth from a mere 13 1/2 million followers to 20 million will occur by the year 2050.

Also, the role of Israel will change. It will continue to be the "homeland" of the Jewish people and of the potentially persecuted. But it will no longer be the receiver of financial and moral support from Jews in Diaspora. Israel will reverse its role and send emissaries overseas to assist struggling Jewish communities with funds, leadership and energy.

Judaism will continue its age old survival mechanism -- adapt to time.

Reflections on Phil Blazer

Phil Blazer is a leading intellectual in the Jewish Community. He has expressed important opinions and positions not only in newspaper commentary, but also on radio and television. The comments he contributed to this book were sent along with graciously expressed enthusiasm about being a part of this book. I find the juxtaposition between his remarks and those of Mr. Caruba (see Health & Science section) is certainly interesting. I hope Mr. Caruba reads the reflections of Mr. Blazer as the two have opposing views on the future of Jewry, while both acknowledging the trend towards inter-marriages.

I find one of Mr. Blazer's most interesting reflections to be his comment that while the orthodox Jewish community has been against proselytizing since the Middle Ages they must inevitably reverse their position in order to combat a population decrease. It is also significant to note Blazer's prediction that Israel will eventually reverse its role and send emissaries overseas to assist with Jewish communities. He points out that the key to all survival is adapting to the times. This is a truly dramatic entry, which I value very much.

FARIDA SHARAN - spiritual thinker

The increased consciousness of our new millennium will allow individuals to be more in touch with themselves, be more interested in the mystery, majesty and power of their being. They will awaken to the clarity reality of cause and effect and want to live correctly, carefully and consciously so they may experience fully their creativity, joy, love and spirituality. Each person will assume self-responsibility for achieving and sharing their best.

Reflections on Farida Sharan

Ms. Sharan has expressed an ideal in her comments that are truly wonderful. It would be terrific if people will come to be more in touch with themselves and the mystery of being, even if the only reason is the coming of a new millennium. There are tremendous mysteries to life. Since the time of our founding fathers there has been astounding advances in communications, medicine and technology, yet there is still no true understanding of why we are here, or how we came to be here. Did it all happen by a single explosion? The Big Bang theory is more mystical, magical and supernatural than any theory I could imagine. Sharan seems to predict that our understanding of life's questions will begin to be answered. Man will go through a reawakening that will cause individuals to live more carefully and conscientiously. If true, the coming century is sure to be a wonderful spiritual occasion.

I truly wish that her Sharan's last comment that each person will assume self-responsibility, will come to fruition. It will be refreshing to find people handling their own messes as opposed to dialing 911 for every calamity in their lives, or blaming their upbringing for their behavior, or even running to the nearest attorney to absolve themselves of responsibility. What a joy the new millennium would be.

FATHER SYLVESTER JOSEPH M. LIVOLS1

I can write of the church in the coming millennium with a very limited view, totally without knowledge of God's Providence. The views and opinions of anyone in the church, in varying degree, are subject to this human, frail, faulty condition. Even so, an army of Catholics, men and women, will rise by the Year 2000 and parade before those susceptible millions of minds who will read or hear their predictions, prophecies and projections of both gloom and glory.

I know for certain that the Catholic Church will not cease to exist, either in the coming millennium or any millennium to come. I am somewhat convinced by many great minds in the church that in the Western World the church will be smaller, perhaps a great deal smaller, than it claims to be today. Indeed, today the true Catholics hardly approach the number that is usually cited.

As a boy in my hometown of Caldwell, Father James Vincent Fitzpatrick repeatedly impressed upon me that "the church is dying in the West" and that the great future for Jesus and his church would be in Africa and Asia. I am convinced these sixty years later that this will happen in America. It is possible, however, that baby boys and girls being born may well turn a growing materialistic America back to its Christian greatness and make even that greatness small in comparison. Remember the wonder of God's mysterious Providence!

In any event, in small pockets of Christians, men ordained to the Priesthood of Jesus throughout our country will gather believers round an altar at which Jesus, our only Priest, will keep his church alive at its very source of grace and spiritual power. Satan, the greatest enemy of mankind, inscrutably permitted by God, may yet cause spiritual and material havoc beyond any prophesy and prediction capable by mere human minds, and certainly by men and women who wittingly or unwittingly leave themselves under his influence. One human person alone stands in his way in the cause of Jesus, and it is a woman -- The Woman who is destined and designed by the Almighty to do so: Mary, The Virgin Mother of Our Savior Jesus, and Mother of the true sons and daughters of His Church.

Reflections on Father Livolsi

I approached a number of religious leaders and public figures including the Reverend Billy Graham, who I have admired through the years. Reverend Graham declined partly because of his health and partly because of the demands of his present lifestyle. I was fortunate to obtain reflections from many other religious leaders. One of my childhood heroes, Bishop Fulton J. Sheen, I am sure would have contributed to this book were he alive today. I came to know Bishop Sheen during the later years of his life as we worked together on some television appearances. He wrote me a beautiful handwritten letter which I prize to this very day. With the absence of Bishop Sheen, I turned to another religious leader who I admire deeply, Father Livolsi.

Father Livolsi built his own church in a quiet section of New Jersey, with the help of local members of his parish. He is an amazing man with a gift of speech. There has never been a speaker more eloquent than he. Those who have had the pleasure of listening to his sermons will agree that he has an absolutely magnetic ability to communicate. He could easily find his way onto television as his compelling hypnotic quality is almost in parallel with my friend, the late Bishop Sheen. I asked Father Livolsi if he would give me his reflections on the future of the Catholic Church and thankfully he agreed. Along with his comments, he wrote me a handwritten note explaining that he prayed over the task and then wrote down the words in one sitting, without corrections or further reflections. I think his thoughts are beautifully expressed and I am so proud they are part of this volume.

MELVIN SLAVICK -- SCULPTOR

Dear Amazing: Thank you for believing in me. Now, about art in the next millennium. I feel that more and more people, old and young, will turn to the field of art as a profession. They will be looking for an alternative to work that is not much more than pushing paper from one desk to another.

People need three things in life to feel happy. First, they need contact with nature of some sort. Second, they need relationships with other humans, and third, they need to feel and be creative. Bringing something to life is one of the greatest feelings on earth.

People will live more simply and devote themselves to their painting, gardening, hobbies, sculpting, cooking and love for each other.

Reflections on Melvin Slavick

I found it fascinating in this book to study the reflections not just of political, legal, psychiatric and scientific minds, but of artists as well. Slavick comments on the three things that people need in life. It is refreshing to hear positive reflections. It is hard to imagine a society existing without the influence and the contributions of people like Slavick.

Slavick had a successful career in the entertainment industry creating sculptures for movies and amusement parks. He decided to end that career at age 30 and began making sculptures for celebrities. His clients have included Disney, Warner Brothers, Universal, and Paramount. He has been commissioned and done personal sculptures of, among others, President Bush, Nancy Reagan, John Travolta, Cher, Nicholas Cage, Colin Powell, Lauren Bacall, Jane Seymore, Jean-Claude Van Damme, Jay Leno, Donald Trump, Charlton Heston, Billy Crystal, Whoopie Goldberg, Tom Arnold, Carol Burnett, Mel Gibson, and yes, even me. Despite his success, he feels most proud that he spent over four years granting nearly 60 wishes for children through the Make-A-Wish Foundation. These are inspiring and beautiful acts. Some people are blessed with gifts in life, and it is wonderful to see him returning some of his success to those that need it.

Slavick's most haunting piece of commentary in his remarks was the quiet praise "that people will live more simply if they devote themselves." Wouldn't that be an ideal.

RAY FERRY - PUBLISHER

No other development of civilization has impacted the evolution of humanity as has publishing. The archiving of knowledge and its mass distribution has provided the foundation upon which civilization has been built. In the next millennium, while many disciplines of society will change, the manner in which knowledge is disseminated will likely experience the earliest and most radical transformations.

Under the influence of a movement initially justified by environmental concerns, the printed word on paper as an expression of ideas will likely disappear completely in favor of electronic media. Early on in the millennium, probably within the first century, publications will be distributed in the form of minuscule disks or chips that will be viewed on portable players in an attempt to recreate the traditional reading experience electronically, but with the ever increasing addition of multimedia embellishments. In short order, all representations of intellectual communication primarily dependant upon the printed word will give way to highly concentrated, interactive multimedia presentations as the level of reading comprehension among the world populace declines. The depiction of alpha-numeric letters will become little more than graphic embellishments to provide visual support to impressions upon the mind. Vocabulary, particularly the visual representation of phonetic symbols, will become truncated to a condensed collection of expressions requiring the least effort to communicate a thought.

Some original paper printed volumes will probably be archived for posterity, but such volumes will not be available to, or be of interest to, the public. Distributed data will likely be purified of politically undesirable content. Ultimately, all "publications," particularly those which are news oriented, will be broadcast via satellite and received directly by a player, permitting the luxury of instantaneous alteration of information.

The Internet as a publishing avenue, will cease to exist in its current form. This is because communications profit interests will not be served by permitting continued unrestricted online access, and, additionally, because the current means of access will be replaced by direct satellite transmission and unauthorized access would be common and interfere with profit. Finally, unrestricted dissemination of ideas and information among the populace will directly threaten the foundation of a "new world order." Thus, the Internet will be controlled as an interactive broadcast medium with tightly regulated content. The youth of the privileged segment of society will likely consider "published" information on the basis of abstract concept and will learn through interaction with virtual reality computers. The lower classes will be placated by increasing entertainment programming.

Reflections on Ray Ferry

Ray Ferry is the editor and publisher of a beautifully mounted magazine called, "Famous Monsters of Filmland." In addition to his own magazine, he has been involved in many other publications in the classic horror fantasy and science fiction genres. In the past year, he devoted two cover stories in his magazine to me -- one dealt with my analysis of great horror movies and their influence on my career and imagination, and the other cover story dealt with my analysis of the use of hypnotism as a theme in many horror or thriller movies.

I have found his entire commentary to be fascinating. As a publisher he contends that the gradual influence of the electronic media will cause sacrifices to the printed word. It is interesting to note his conjecture that we will receive publication chips that will be viewed on portable players, making the printed word give way to multimedia presentations. It is somewhat sad that while original paper printed volumes will be stored for posterity, they may not be available, or even of interest, to the public. Somehow, while I believe his thoughts are true, I cannot imagine not being able to hold a book in my hand and turn the pages. His prediction that the Internet as a publishing revenue source will cease to exist is fascinating. The concept that the Internet will not serve the profit interests is thought provoking. Read his remarks about the future of the written word and wonder how we could adjust to it were it to take place tomorrow.

ROBERT COLLINS - PUBLISHER

Newspapers will be alive and well in the next millennium. The difference, though, will probably be the way people receive their home delivered paper.

There will come a time when newspapers will be electronically transmitted to the home and have content that reflects the specific news interests of that particular household.

At this point, it's difficult to say in what form readers will receive the news. It's certainly possible that pages similar to what the reader sees today will be printed in the home or they will have the opportunity to scan pages on a terminal or television screen and print out information that they care to keep or take along with them.

Television and newspapers will continue to compete as they have in the past, but here again, in my view, newspapers will have a decided edge in that they can create a product design based on the personal interests of the reader.

Reflections on Robert Collins

Bob Collins has been a long time friend of mine and one of the most remarkable newspapermen I have ever known. In addition to being President and Editor of the Asbury Park Press, he has through the years had large sections of the Gannett newspaper organization under his helm. I consider him the perfect troubleshooter. He can walk into a newspaper organization that is on a shaky foundation and build it into a dynamic and powerful success. He clearly reminds me of what I envision as the newspapermen of a bygone era. You saw them in black and white movies -- dynamic, strong willed, determined, and blessed with the integrity to withstand the pressures of commercial interests trying to alter an editorial decision. I cannot imagine Bob Collins being bought out by any source other than his conscience.

It is reassuring to see that he feels the newspaper will survive. I suppose there will be a day when we will not hear the thud of the newspaper boy tossing the paper from his bicycle. I worry about the day when we will not be able to turn the pages of the newspaper as we wish. To think that all of this will be done electronically is not the most reassuring feeling. I think there is something to be said for holding the page. Of course, Bob mentions that we can print out those pages that we want, and the electronic version will allow us to turn immediately to find our favorite sections. However, often as one pages through the paper to a favorite section, you notice an article that catches your eye. Using an electronic alternative these article might be overlooked. Is it possible to imagine the traditional newspaper being absent from our society? I pray that will not happen.

NICK MEGLIN - editor, Mad Magazine

As far as editing "MAD" is concerned, the most important software programming we are developing is called "Laugh-Check." Similarly to any spell-check program, it rejects all gags it deems "not funny." Oops, maybe MAD best dump this program! We'll never get out an issue if it really works!

Reflections on Nick Meglin

Nick Meglin is a satirical editor for MAD Magazine. He has lampooned your truly in comics of the past. His prediction of a "Laugh-Check" is interesting. We are seemingly entering an age where computers are similar to HAL in the movie 2001: A Space Odyssey. Computers are learning to think the way their programmers think. There is little doubt in my mind that someone in the next decade will offer such a service where the software will be in a position to judge whether certain material is funny or not.

I can see this software program being used by gag writers for Jay Leno, Jerry Seinfeld or David Letterman. My only concern is that bosses might cut back on the hours contributed by gag writers. They might even dare to cutback on the amount of gag writers on a team. Perish the though of big business entering the comic field!

JULIUS LA ROSA - fired by Godfrey

La Rosa's firing by Godfrey forever changed both Godfrey's and La Rosa's careers. LaRosa went on to a successful career in singing, as well as that of disc jockey. I asked the singer for his reflections for the world of acting and performing in the next millennium.

His response: Politicians will get out of the Business!

DAVID MEYER - publisher

Conjuring, which includes magic, legerdemain, hocus pocus, and sleight of hand, has existed in the 20th Century primarily as a hobby and amateur entertainment. The stars in the industry, such as David Copperfield, can be counted on two hands. Yet its enthusiasts, numbering many thousands, thrive in a microcosmic "magic world" that is sustained by its own societies, suppliers, and in vast printed literature which explains tricks and memorializes performers. What magic books of the 21st century will be like, perhaps only Kreskin knows.

Reflections on David Meyer

David Meyer and I shared a friendship with the legendary Hearst newspaperman Bob Lund. Lund was neither a performer of magic, nor a creator of magical techniques. However, his collection of thousands upon thousands of pieces of memorabilia made him one of the great authorities on conjuring in the world. Meyer and my shared friendship with Lund brought us together. Meyer is an equally brilliant authority on the history and practice of conjuring. Like Lund, Meyer is not a performer, nor does he invent magical mysteries, but his editorship of the private journal Magicol, has made him a legend in the conjuring industry. Meyer also published the writings of the legendary South American magician David Bamburg. The book is perhaps the most honest, realistic autobiography ever written on what it takes to survive as a great magician.

In addition to the reputation Meyer has built in the world of conjuring, he has also become one of the authoritative publishers on herbs and folk medicine. His interest in the field goes back to his grandfather who in the first decade of this century was investigating many of the natural products that can be found in today's health food stores.

I asked Meyer to comment on the magic books of the future and I found his reflections interesting. He is in a unique position as publisher of Magicol to know what secrets are passed around in book form. As far back as history will tell, the sorcerer's apprentice guarded the secrets of his teacher's craft. Books containing techniques and methods were found only in the hands of the few, were written for very few, and were very guarded. My suspicion is that magic books in the next millennium will be pretty much the same as they have been for the last four or five hundred years -- guarded tomes for masters of the craft. I began my career as a magician at age nine and I began performing at age eleven. My interest in the craft's literature has been intense since my childhood, and I have come to the same conclusion as Meyer -- there will be little change in magic books in the future.

FREDERIK POHL - Science Fiction Writer

One of the local Chicago newspapers asked me to name five things which will no longer be around in the year 2210. 1 said, "There will not be any computers, television sets, traffic jams, hospitals or airports." That I am pretty sure of. Whatever else happens depends a great deal on what people make happen.

There have been many attempts by bright and well-informed people to figure out methodologies for forecasting the future. They figured out a whole bunch of really snazzy ones: Delphi Herman Kahn scenario writing, methodological mapping, trend line extrapolations, etc. All had one thing in common -- none of them worked.

A man named Dennis Gabor, who is best known for inventing the hologram, is also one of the leaders in the future studies discipline. He summarized it all when he said, "It is impossible to predict the future, the best we can do is invent it." You really can't say much about what will be in the 21st or 22nd Century, you can only say what can be and what may be. There are certain things that there won't be, like the five I mentioned.

Reflections on Frederik Pohl

I have always had a love affair with science fiction. At the same time, I have recognized that in their writings, science fiction authors have "foreseen" the future evolution of technology. Modern travel and communications are but two examples of "predictions" that came to pass that can be found in the early science fiction works. During the Second World War, the comic strip Buck Rogers was occasionally censored because it introduced concepts and machinations that were on the mind of some of our military strategists. In early horror science fiction writing, Mary Shelley warned us through her Frankenstein monster that science could taper too greatly with nature trying to produce or create humans. Today we find it possible to decide on the sex of an unborn child. So, perhaps Pohl's remarks are accurate when he says that the best we can do with the future is invent it.

I can't help but be intrigued by Pohl's statement that "around the year 2210 there will no longer be any computers." I surely hope that his statement about the five areas that will no longer exist will remain clearly in print and this book will still exist a few hundred years from now. He certainly has been more direct and more specific in targeting his predictions than anything Nostradamus ever said. I wish I could be here in the year 2210.

RUTH STAFFORD PEALE - magazines

Magazines will be very important in the next millennium. Life will be fast-paced and all kinds of information will be available. The future magazine will be about twenty-five pages of a small sized pamphlet or booklet using few words and lots of signs or symbols or drawings. A good title for such a publication might be, "This Tells It All."

Reflections on Ruth Stafford Peale

Ruth Stafford Peale is Chairman of Guideposts, Inc. She reflects that magazines in the new millennium will consist of smaller sizes and less pages. She predicts that the publications will rely on signs and symbols, suggesting that words will be too limiting. Instead of an entire paragraph, the thought will be expressed with a single drawing or sign. I gather we will have little time for expanded verbiage. I wonder if the person reading these booklets will have time to smell the roses.

BARRY A. MILLER - Editor, Lotto World

Here are my views about the future of the lottery business in the 21st Century:

1.   Every state except Utah, Hawaii and Nevada will have a state lottery.

2.   Lottery players will play the lottery at home, via the Internet, television, or home computer. Though state lotteries oppose the concept of Internet play, they will come around once they realize the Internet opens a world-wide market for them.

3.   Interactive lottery games such as Bingo, Keno and Quick Draw will become more popular as people play at home. Daily large jackpot Lotto games will be developed.

4.   Instant tickets, also called scratch offs, will be played via Internet, television or the home computer with an in-house device that prints scratch-off tickets in your home.

5.   Jackpot prizes for regular Lotto-type games will increase to $200 million or more.

6.   Lotteries will offer trips, merchandise and prizes in addition to money.

7.   More states will band together with multi-state games to compete with the larger states who can offer large jackpots.

8.   The states will offer their own versions of lottery clubs giving the public a chance to join with other players in buying tickets. This will increase the buying power of each player and increase his or her chances of winning lottery prizes.

9.   Each lottery player will be able to obtain a full and complete statistical package based on past lottery drawings. This package can be customized to fit any player's need to reflect his or her best lottery strategy.

10.   Foreign lottery play will be available to American players via the Internet, television and home computer. Countries will join together to offer jackpots of enormous proportions.

11.   New and better lottery playing strategies will be developed to help players win.

12.   Statisticians and mathematicians who once scoffed at seeking ways to cut the odds of winning lottery jackpots will turn their attention to the lottery.

13.   The state lotteries will continue their efforts at making the games a random experience by developing new technologies for lottery drawings, including electronic random number selection. Machines blowing balls into tubes will be discontinued as a number selection method.

14.   All drawings will be televised.

15.   A 24-hour lottery television network will be formed offering statistics, strategies, tips and features on the lottery.

16.   Most states will earmark their lottery revenues for specific needs such as education, services for the elderly, services for the poor, etc.

Reflections on Barry Miller

I have known Barry Miller for years. His magazine has honored me by featuring me on the cover twice. He has given me a close understanding of how popular the lottery has become in the United States. Miller suggests that the lottery will progress to people playing at home through electronic devices. There seems little doubt that this is going to take place as there are already trends in this area. For instance, Internet gambling is thriving with casino type games. It once again demonstrates the expansion of gambling in our society. I find it fascinating that Miller speculates that lottery jackpots will grow to $200 million dollars. Every time I hear of some individual winning many millions of dollars I wonder if it would somehow make more sense to divide these huge jackpots among many winners. In a jackpot of $100 million dollars, you could bring magic to the lives of 25 or 30 people instead of just one by giving each winner 3 or 4 million, instead of one winner taking home all 100 million. I assume suddenly winning 3 or 4 million dollars should be enough for anyone.

Miller's suggestion that mathematical minds will seek ways of helping people win is very intriguing. This is certainly the case in many casino games, with blackjack being an obvious example. Mathematicians have been a source of advice in how best to handle strategy at the gaming tables, so it seems logical that they would eventually apply their knowledge to the lottery industry.

The thought of a twenty-four hour lottery network is also very interesting. It seems like an awful lot of hours to devote to one topic, but then again we have heard mentioned scores of times in recent months that mankind is going to be "gifted" with over 500 channels on our television. Maybe enough is enough.

JOHN ROMERO - Marketing and Gaming

Authority

With the World Wide Web growing to five billion users by 2010, e-mail will replace the telephone, fax and direct mail as the favored method by which casinos communicate with their regular customers.

Later in the century, by 2015, casinos will rediscover the selling power of personal letters, followed by a swing back to "snail mail."

Cost savings from Internet marketing will offset declining room rates brought about by a glut of new casinos in Las Vegas. After a slump, the city will blossom again in 2020, emerging as the world's number one visitor destination.

Mississippi will emerge as the number one gambling state and Tunica and the Gulf Coast will emerge as a strong contender to Las Vegas.

New slot machines will carry on conversations with players.

All casinos will switch to coin-free slot machines. The "iron triangle" of drop bucket to counting room to coin fills will vanish, saving casinos millions in labor and equipment. Instead of dropping coins in trays, the machines will print winners a check.

Gambling in the US will suffer a momentary setback as opponents describe it as an "addiction." But a backlash by consumers who view it as entertainment will allow growth to surge again.

Huge casinos will fall in popularity, replaced by smaller, more opulent and compact casinos that will attract customers through highly personal treatment and superb accommodations at bargain prices.

Reflections on John Romero

After knowing John Romero for over 30 years, I consider him one of the most remarkable entrepreneurs I have ever known. He was on the cutting edge of society when the explosion of popularity of gambling in the United States hit. He has been a consultant to the gambling industry in the area of marketing for years. As a matter of fact, he is currently completing a book entitled, "Secrets of Casino Marketing." John Romero popularized gaming tournaments all over the world. These tournaments would be sponsored by the casinos and bring in high rollers from all over to play for large jackpots. Romero also has a monthly column simply titled "Marketing' in a wagering business magazine. He truly has an intuitive feel of where the gaming industry is moving and I think his predictions are highly significant.

It is interesting to see that he picks Mississippi of all places to be the future number one gambling state. Throughout my life, Las Vegas has been the gambling capitol of the world, so this prediction is surprising. I recently finished a run at a casino in Mississippi and was impressed by the wide range of hometowns of casino guests. The customers literally came from all over the country, and in some cases other parts of the world. I was also impressed with the graciousness and the personalization of the staff at the casinos. They made people feel very much at home and comfortable, as opposed to being simply part of a machine.

It is interesting that Romero does not avoid the critics of the gaming industry who describe gambling as an addiction. However, he is quick to point out that the consumers will revolt against any gambling restrictions now that they have learned to accept gambling as a form of entertainment. Romero also predicts that huge casinos will diminish in popularity and be replaced by smaller and personalized bargain settings. I would be willing to bet $1,000 at this moment that not only will that prediction come true, but it will come true long before the year 2010.

John Romero recently did a story about me in his column titled, "The Night They Dealt To Kreskin." People ask me about how well I do in casinos, and I have been banned by many casinos, especially in Las Vegas. In fact, I have been told by a number of dealers that my picture appeared for years in the rogues gallery of every casino in Las Vegas. However, the banning seems to have gone by the wayside in recent years. I still gamble, as I have for years, in Reno and Tahoe. I love to go to some of the smaller casinos in Las Vegas and Atlantic City. I usually play my favorite game, blackjack. It was a recent event at a blackjack table that lead Romero to write his recent column.

I have made it a policy not to gamble at the casino at which I am appearing, so I usually find a different casino each night to spend some time in. Gambling for me is not a compulsion, but I do find blackjack to be a wonderful way of taking my mind off the pressures and intensity of my professional work as a mind reader. One particular night in Atlantic City, I entered the Resorts Casino. I had $300 on me and I sat down at about eleven o'clock. I play a very conservative game of blackjack and one day I might even write a book on how I win. But on this night, after two hours of play, I had lost about $200 and I was tired. I turned to my road manager and told him I was going to play with just $30 and then go back to my room.

The game of blackjack today is a serious challenge to the player, mainly because casinos are using eight decks in a shoe. The game was never meant to be eight decks. It was invented as a four deck game by John Scarne in the 1960's. With eight decks, blackjack is just about the worst game you can play in a casino. Roulette and Baccarat have almost a 50/50 chance of winning, and even craps has better odds than eight-deck blackjack. However, for me, there is a certain allure to blackjack. Parenthetically, I predict there will be more and more casinos offering four deck blackjack games in spite of the fear of players counting cards. As casinos proliferate all over the country, casinos will have to appeal to players by making the games more tempting with better odds.

With the eight-deck shoe, a dealer can sometimes go an entire shoe without busting - that is going over 21 and losing. The reason is that with eight decks there are so many little cards in the deck, the dealer, being the last hand to play, has a good chance of hitting under 21 without busting from an oversupply of high cards. Back at my blackjack game, it was one in the morning when I started with my $30 dollars. An hour and twenty minutes later, the table was surrounded by some 70 people, including security guards, off duty pit people, dealers, tourists, and players. In an eight deck shoe, you are lucky to win three or four hands in a row. Five or six wins is an excellent run. After playing for an hour and twenty minutes, much to the screaming delight of the people around me, I had won twenty-one hands in a row. The casino said I had won over $4,000 dollars in that time. It was actually much more than that, as I had been giving away money to well wishers, as the chips began to look like monopoly pieces. Finally, one of the pit people said, "Kreskin - cash the rest in. The people you are giving all this money to are just going to blow it again." They assigned a guard to me and I was escorted, along with my road manager, to our car. The odds of winning twenty-one hands in a row must be around impossible to one. I do know that a few years earlier, in Las Vegas, I left Harrah's were I was performing and went to another casino. There were reports on NBC the next day of my streak of sixteen straight blackjack wins in a row.

The question of winning at blackjack always turns to my ability to perceive thoughts. Does this ability give me an advantage in the game? My answer is no, my skills as a mentalist do not aid me in the playing of blackjack. Perhaps if the dealer glanced at his down card, I could perceive what he was thinking. But dealers simply do not do this anymore except to check for a blackjack. I cannot read the thoughts of a playing card that no one is consciously aware of.

For years, my dentist, who is a brilliant poker player, has encouraged me to play poker. The question then is would I cheat or not cheat. I'd like to say I wouldn't, but poker is a game in which you use all your skills to handle your opponent. All of my skills cannot be used in blackjack.

REGIS PHILBIN

The networks will decline in power. Cable gains will continue because of the fragmentation of viewership. I believe the overall quality of television will decline as well - there will be just too many stations. I think this probably parallels the continued "dumbing down of America." It's too bad and I hope I'm wrong, but that is what I see in the future.

Reflections on Regis Philbin

I owe a debt of gratitude to Regis Philbin for all the years that he has been supportive of my work and for the enthusiasm he has expressed. What you see in Regis is what you get -- whether he is on camera or off, whether the microphone is live or turned off. The real Regis is the Regis you see every morning on television. He is a dynamic, inquisitive, refreshing character with a wonderful sense of humor and a tremendous zest for life. He truly cherishes the success of his career and certainly doesn't take it for granted. He works very hard to make each show special. He never stops observing his surroundings so he can comment with Kathie Lee on the show the next morning.

Not too many years ago, Regis called and asked me if my mother would appear on his show. My mother is not a professional performer and has never sought the limelight, so she was very nervous about her appearance. The treatment of my mother was so beautifully handled that I'm not sure she realized when the camera started and when it ended. Regis was graceful and reassuring. The only time my mother became anxious was when the crew put makeup on her and tried to attach a microphone to her suit. She couldn't understand why she needed any more makeup and why the contraption was being wound around her. Regis was able to calm her with a few simple comments. He got her talking and brought out a natural feeling of relaxation. Once the camera rolled, Regis was true to form and asked her a number of sundry questions such as, "What did Kreskin do that was amazing as a child?" My mother is inexperienced at the anecdotal traditions of talk show television and simply said, "Oh, many things." Regis followed with, "Was there something special that you remember?" My mother answered, "A lot of things." I was not on the set -- Regis made sure that I was put away in the control room. I wondered as the segment went by how the viewers had taken my mother's appearance. My mother hadn't added much in detail to Regis' questions but I heard from countless viewers in the weeks and months that followed that my mother had come across graciously and that there seemed to be a wonderful quality between Regis and her. The viewers didn't care about the content of my mothers remarks and simply remembered glowingly the treatment and joy that seemed to flow during the interview. I credit the entire event to the very gifted Regis Philbin.

His remarks on the future of broadcasting do not surprise me. What impresses me is that he was so absolutely frank in his commentary. He didn't hold back on one negative thought. The man is simply too honest to conceal his true opinions. Anyone who has ever asked him a question knows this quality about him. I thank him for his contribution to this book, and for the remarkable support he has given to all of my endeavors throughout the years.

Arthur Godfrey - Talk Show host

I only came to know Godfrey in the latter years of his career. His peak had passed and he was a shadow of the once great titan of broadcasting. Even so, his reflections in the early 1960's are interesting.

He predicted that the desk and sofa talk show that he created and popularized would become a thing of the past. The concept of guests appearing on a television show to converse or perform for the host would disappear. The sophistication of television productions would create a demand for perfection and necessitate that all shows would be scripted and pre-recorded. He felt the public would stop accepting an informal, less structured television production. At the time, considerable attention was given to his remarks because he was forecasting the end of his creation.

Reflections on Arthur Godfrey

Godfrey was proved wrong. It is tragic that he made the remarks, and perhaps he did so out of bitterness or because he was losing his understanding of an industry in which he once enjoyed a staggering amount of control. However, his influence on the development of broadcasting is unchallenged. I often say to university students who are studying communications that if they have not learned and discussed the Arthur Godfrey phenomena then their courses have been woefully inadequate. Godfrey was such a powerful force that he was actually chosen to lead the United States! During the 1950's, with the Red scare looming, the federal government developed contingency plans for handling an atomic attack. It had been quietly decided that if the President, Vice President, and the normal succession had been killed or rendered unavailable, Godfrey would lead the country until the military was able to restore order and hold elections. When I first talked of this fact, I was laughed at. However, this fact has been confirmed in a Time Magazine story. There was a recording made with calming instructions that was to be played over radio and television until Godfrey could get to the microphone and guide the public. The reason Godfrey was chosen for this assignment is clear - he was the most trusted and respected person in America. Conventional wisdom holds that if Godfrey had run, he would have been elected President of the United States.

Godfrey didn't sing well, but he did sing on his show and he loved to play his ukulele, even though he wasn't much better at it than he was at singing. He did what made him happy. He even tried a couple of quick dances, even though he was partially crippled from an auto accident. When he was at his peak, he was masterful. His genius was he knew what his audience was thinking. He restructured broadcasting, from television to radio. To this day there is neither talk show nor a live radio broadcast that doesn't owe a debt of gratitude to Godfrey. One of the key changes he made in the industry was based on his theory that there was no need to speak with pontifical austerity and formality on the air. Godfrey reasoned that if there were more than one person in a room, they were probably conversing. His theory followed that most of his audience listened or watched alone. Therefore, by losing the formality of the traditional style, and speaking as if he were addressing only one person, a stronger connection could be made. And he was right. This new way of speaking created bonds with individuals in the viewing/listening audience. People felt connected to Godfrey. They trusted him and they liked him. The downfall began when he fired one of his singers on the air. The on-air firing was intentional, and had the backing of the CBS brass, but it troubled the American public. They viewed the firing as disloyal to a family member. Godfrey lost a measure of trust he had worked so hard to develop.

Godfrey's prediction for the downfall of the talk show was wrong. If anything, there are more people in broadcasting today trying to imitate him than ever before. In most cases, however, the imitators are unsuccessful.

STEVE ALLEN - Humorist, Musician, Author, Raconteur

Regarding what changes "could possibly" lie ahead in the world of comedy in the next millennium I would think that the first reaction to the approach and arrival of the year 2000 will be simply a good many jokes on the general subject.

Predictions are one thing, of course, and hopes or recommendations are quite another. I would hope that the trend of the last 20 years or so, towards an ever-increasing emphasis on vulgarity and sleaze would finally wear out its welcome and that there might be a return to true wit and comedic insight on the part of at least our more creative practitioners of the comic arts, whether writers or performers.

The approach of the millennium itself - alas - will no doubt bring about a sharp increase in the sort of goofola popular thinking currently so common. In an age when there are more technological means of communication than our forefathers could have dreamed of, when we receive data from radio, television, the print media, the Internet, and the lecture platform, it might have been anticipated that we would be the best-informed generation in history and that we might also have been moderately instructed in the methods of rational thinking, or at the least the exercise of simple common sense.

Precisely the opposite, of course, is what we now witness. Whether there is a God or not, it happens to be the case that while the traditional churches are experiencing declines in their numbers, the more bizarre forms of belief are flourishing. The interest in conclusive evidence, for at least many, seems to be a thing of the past, and there is apparently no philosophical assertion too bizarre that it will not enlist the interest of considerable numbers of followers.

Our professional humorists and comedians now have the opportunity to say something constructive about the present degree of belief in astronomy, tarot cards, alien invasions and abductions, the power of pyramids, crystals, linoleum-chips – whatever. All of this should be target material for those who think in funny ways. Here's hoping they will bend to the task.

Reflections on Steve Allen

Steve Allen is a genius. In the days of live television, Allen hosted *The Tonight Show* and night after night demonstrated his incredible wit. He could create entertaining shows out of some of the most inane situations and some of the strangest guests that have ever appeared on television. For example, he had guests that would demonstrate how far they could stretch their tongues, and people who could twist objects into strange shapes. Allen has always possessed the ability to see the wild, bizarre side of humor and bring it to the mainstream national audience. Yet even with his gifted sense of humor, one of his true secrets of success was his serious discussions at the beginning of each program. I remember one night where his topic was crime and the show went to such depths, that the program's normal hour and forty-five minutes had to be extended. While the world initially embraced Allen for his humor, he is much more than a comedian. He is a masterful musician and accomplished pianist. He composed the song "Picnic" as well as his theme song, "This Could Be The Start Of Something Big." He is a wonderful social commentator and has written an incredible array of books from novels to a non-fiction piece that analyzed white-collar crime to a heart wrenching commentary on the period of his life when his son became a member of a cult. He is one of the scholars of modem society.

I owe Allen a debt of gratitude because in the early 60's he offered me my first opportunity to perform on national television. It was a wonderful break and he gave me nearly twenty minutes of airtime. I was introduced as Kreskin, as it was before the word "Amazing" had been added to my name. Humor surrounds Allen, and my appearance that night was no exception. I remember being introduced and beginning to walk out onto the stage. As it was my first television appearance, I was not used to the pathways towards the curtain or the brightness of the network television lights. I walked out, bowed and then turned to walk over to Allen to shake his hand. As I reached the elevated desk platform, I tripped over my own feet. That trip was my debut into the world of television, and it became quite famous. For years, Johnny Carson did a comedy bit called "Carnac; the Magnificent" in which he played a mentalist. Each time Carson performed the routine, he would trip on his way out to the stage. This routine was based on me and the time I tripped during my first television appearance.

As for Allen's comments for this book, notice that in his analysis of humor he introduces serious topics. He points out the decline in the attendance of traditional churches and a corresponding increase in bizarre beliefs. What this actually suggests must be left to the sociologists and philosophers. The trouble with sociologists, however, is that they are rarely able to expand to the future, instead explaining why things already happened. I am not sure that is the best contribution that can be given to society.

ART LINKLETTER - Television Legend

The advertising dollars, which dictate what shows stay on or go off, will undergo an astounding change due to the emerging "older" audience.

Today the magic numbers are 18-39. By 2050, one in every four adults will be over 65 and the ratings will favor shows that appeal to an aging America.

In the last century we have added 30 years to the average life. This will continue to change the make-up of sponsor dollars. Unbelievable!

- Art Linkletter, President, UCLA Center on Aging

Reflections on Art Linkletter

Art Linkletter makes the prediction that a remarkable shift in television and broadcast fair will occur in the new millenium. Linkletter correctly asserts that television programming is beholden to the advertising dollar, and advertisers will be going after the largest segment of the viewing audience - those over 65 years of age. As a result, broadcasters will create content that caters to the older members of American Society.

Art Linkletter is a senior citizen who continues to stay very active, conducting lectures before organizations and business groups. In my lifetime, I have found no one person who was as articulate and able to communicate with anyone on any subject as Art Linkletter. From his days as the host of his daily CBS television show House Party through to today, Linkletter has proved to be a master at communicating with all walks of life. He has the ability to discuss topics on a humorous level or on an intellectual level or anywhere in between. He can also craft an intriguing conversation with any age group. He made communicating with children respectable. He created priceless moments on his television show asking youngsters their opinions and reflections on life. He is truly a master communicator.

His powerful communication techniques, without the use of four letter words or sexually suggestive phraseology, came from his deep understanding of human nature. He was an orphan who chose never to find his original parents because of the huge debt of gratitude he felt for those who did bring him up. Through this nontraditional upbringing, he sampled many avenues of life, which enabled him to experience relationships with people of ranging lifestyles. He developed the ability to read people quickly.

These abilities were the power behind his television shows. As an example, during the segments with children, Linkletter quickly realized that parents were attempting to influence their children's responses on the show. Once a child was picked by his school principal, the parents would make a point to watch Linkletter's show, specifically the kid segment at the end. They would see the responses kids gave and then coach their own children what subjects not to talk about. Linkletter instinctively knew this was happening and developed a wonderful way to break down this barrier. He would simply ask the child what his parents had asked him, not to talk about! I remember the day one child was asked this question and he matter-of-factly responded "My daddy works for the FBI." The laughter roared through the studio into my living room.

The most remarkable bit of information I ever heard Linkletter extract was again innocent. He was interviewing a child who was around six years old. Linkletter asked the child how she slept, expecting the typical responses, "With my teddy bear," or, "in a princess bed." Instead, this child said she "slept with mommy, except on Thursdays when Uncle came over and then she slept in the living room." The laughter was so hysterical. What could Linkletter do? He just laid down on the floor of the set and sent the show off to commercial. Those were the days that proved the wonder of live television. Perhaps the shows weren't perfect, as taped sitcoms and movies are today, but they were spontaneous. They had life, and a certain edge to them. Except for sporting events and some news coverage, there is so little that is spontaneous today. A show like Linkletter's, while not as polished and antiseptic as today's television, had something extra - it had the promise of the unexpected. Linkletter was a master at capturing and leveraging that.

BUDDY HACKETT - Comedian

Comedy never changes. In the past decade, more language of the street has been used, on stage and off. People set the trend and the funny people bend it a bit more.

The jokes will stay the same, but the method might change, for instance, computer heckling might start. There might be computer testing of punch lines. But, what's the difference, there are no more "Hacketts" in the wings.

Reflections on Buddy Hackett

I was delighted to receive a response with commentary from Buddy Hackett. I have always found him to be a naturally funnyman. I remember first being introduced to his humor watching him appear on Jack Paar's show. He wove hilarious stories about slices of life, with perspectives on people he knew. His anecdotes were delivered so naturally, and were so funny, that the home audience, as well as Jack Paar, his studio audience and celebrities on the show were in hysterics.

Buddy comments that in the past decade more language of the street has been used in comedy. I find that Hackett certainly contributed to that trend, much before the current crop of cable network comedians. Appearing in Vegas, Hackett has always posted a sign outside the theater warning that children were not allowed into the show. Language aside, Hackett is a naturally funny man. Without a single blue word or expression, he can quickly cause one to recoil in laughter. Through his live performances and his many movies, Hackett has always helped the public to laugh.

One interesting experience I had with Hackett occurred in Las Vegas. I had finished a performance at a major hotel and was walking through the casino when I bumped into Hackett. We got to talking and he told me that his son was a blackjack dealer at the hotel. We walked over to his son's table and Hackett had me sit down and play. I didn't play long, as I did not feel I was in a winning situation - the deck just didn't seem to be in my favor. However, this was the only time I have ever been in Buddy's presence when I have not heard an onslaught of social commentaries that brought laughter to my eyes and mind. During the game, Hackett simply remained silent and intrigued. He is truly an interesting man, and a huge talent.

PHYLLIS DILLER - Comedian

Dear Kreskin,

I hear of you as we pass like ships in the night. You have a fine reputation as a performer and as a person.

Your request for a quote got into a stack of mail while I was traveling.

It is such a deep and serious question or I would have come up with the answer the day it arrived.

"The millennium, schmillennium. The taste in entertainment will never change. Technology changes but it will always be Wine, Women and Song, or put another way: Tits and Ass."

Love

Phyllis

Reflections on Phyllis Diller

To only say that Diller is funny is doing her an injustice. She is a remarkable individual who has a passion for the philosophy of positive thinking. Indeed, some years ago, a book entitled "The Magic Of Believing" had a special edition reflecting how it had influenced Diller. She has lectured to groups on the power of positive thought and lives what she preaches. Even still, she Is a damn funny woman.

A number of years ago, we were part of a program celebrating Bob Hope's 80th Birthday. Diller and I flew in two days early to attend a charity dinner for one of Mr. Hope's charities. Sometimes cocktail and dinner parties can be dull and shallow. No one could possibly say that about a party that included Phyllis Diller. Before this function I had heard stories of how Diller would liven up parties, but I had never seen her in action. This particular evening, I was sitting at my table conversing with dinner guests about mostly trivial topics. All of a sudden I heard a frightening scream. I jumped up and looked toward the table next to me just in time to hear Diller laughing in the style that is recognized by audiences the world over. It seems that Diller collects rubber animals, such as spiders and ants. If she finds a party to be dragging, she likes to liven things up by dropping one of these giant rubber critters in the food of a fellow guest. I suspect dinner parties all over the world have heard a startling scream of horror followed by the familiar laugh of Phyllis Diller.

DAVID BRENNER - Comedian

In my opinion, and according to the crystal ball which I purchased on the comer of Canal and Mott Streets from a man wearing a soiled turban in the fall of 1993, comedy will change in the following ways in the next millennium:

1   TV Situation Comedies will become funny again.

2. There will be a rash of jokes about the President of the United States and a sheep he kept in the Oval Office.

3. Comedians will no longer ask audience members where they are from and what they do.

4. HBO will once again become TV.

5. Laugh tracks will be outlawed, reducing the number of comedy writers in Los Angeles to seven.

6. The ancestors of David Letterman and Jay Leno will join forces for a nightly, marathon talk show, including a hilarious Top 100 bit.

7. The last man in America to never have his own talk show will be given his own talk show.

8. Businessmen will still be known as "suits" but will not be allowed to decide what is funny, what isn't and what the public wants, passing this responsibility onto creative people and comedians.

9. Minority group comedians will drop four letter words from their acts and become brilliantly funny on merit.

10. The number of persons, male and female, earning a living from stand-up comedy will increase to 107,325,098 and then drop to 92, when a law is passed that one has to be original and truly funny, in order to get a comedy performance license.

11. Americans will no longer think that a woman on TV telling the public that she is sleeping with her priest and his German Shepherd dog is funny, ringing the knell for these kinds of shows and sending Springer Network into Chapter Eleven.

12. The Presidents on Mount Rushmore will be replaced with Johnny Carson, Richard Pryor, Steve Martin and Soupy Sales.

13. Germany will produce its first stand-up comedian.

14. Twenty-three percent of the American public will be alive past the age of 100 and CBS will corner the market.

15. Re-runs of Gilligan's Island will end and twenty-seven never-before-seen Honeymooners will be found.

16. Richard Nixon will be inducted into the Comedy Hall of Fame.

17. Someone else will be ripping off Lenny Bruce's routines.

18. Research will prove that 20th Century comedians who pontificated about national and international news events were no better informed than any butcher in any local supermarket.

19. A comedian's career will be destroyed. by his continual public insistence that the new millenium should start on January 1, 3001, not 3000, repeating the tragic end of the 20th Century comedian who said the same of January 1, 2001, versus 2000.

20. A comedian will break David Brenner's record of 82,678,956 talk show appearances. Rioting will break out in Philadelphia, PA and Guam. David will come out of retirement and make his 82,678,958th appearance to regain the record. Rioting will continue in Guam for unknown reasons.

Reflections on David Brenner

David Brenner has been a part of my life during my entire career as a professional mentalist. He has always had a rather fascinating way of reflecting on life's' experiences. In many ways his humor is that of social commentary, taking us beyond a mere smile to the outward laughter that only comes when our funny bones are severely touched.

He loves to recount a story of a mentalist he was appearing with on a school campus. The mentalist had his paycheck hidden by the audience, with the understanding that if he did not find it, he would forfeit his fee for appearing. The mentalist read the thoughts of the audience and found the check, but then after the show, the mentalist couldn't remember where he parked his own car. Brenner always prefaces the story with the comment, "No, it isn't Kreskin!" However, I remember appearing with Brenner at the campus and losing my car.. I not only couldn't remember where I parked it, but I began to think it might have been stolen.

Some of Brenner's remarks brought quiet chuckles to me as I read them in the privacy of my library. I particularly liked Number 5, where he predicts laugh tracks will be outlawed. That would be a welcome change. With Number 10, I enjoyed the commentary he masks in humor when he estimates the increase in the number of comics, and then the drastic decrease when they have to be funny. I also look forward to his prediction Number 11 coming true, the end of trash television. I have decided to keep David Brenner's 20 Predictions on my desk. Not merely to calculate which of them comes true, but to have a laugh if the day grows gray.

KATHIE LEE GIFFORD

I see nothing but change ahead. As more and more options become available, the industry will become more fragmented. The glory days are over, when audiences would set aside specific times to watch specific shows. Now the only thing predictable is the unpredictability, as the industry scrambles to keep pace with technology. There are already too many talk shows, too many newsmagazines, too many bad sitcoms, and too many all-news channels. I suggest going back to an old-fashioned concept guaranteed to satisfy: READING!

Reflections on Kathie Lee Gifford

Kathie Lee Gifford is a remarkable figure in the entertainment scene today. It is a Herculean task to create an hour of television daily, and Kathie Lee does it with grace. Her banter each day with Regis Philbin on their talk show is an industry standard and Kathie's talent is apparent on the program. The strongest part of the program are the early minutes where, without a script, Kathie Lee and Regis comment on their personal activities, social stresses and the passing scene. They don't always agree, but these spirited conversations have the spice of intrigue.

She is remarkable for the strength of her personality. She was faced with media generated personal problems as well as business intrusions over which she had no control, and she came forth a winner. She is to be admired as a tremendously strong woman, both in her professional life as well as her family life.

Her remarks about the changes she sees taking place in the television industry really hit home. She states that the glory days are over, which I find to be a refreshing and honest commentary. Gifford lists a number of areas where there are already too many television programs and I wonder how the problem can avoid getting worse when the quantity of channels available rises into the four hundred to five hundred range. I love her concluding remark about turning to books for entertainment. I read four books a night, and if the inundation of visual stimuli, i.e. bad television programming, continues, maybe I'll turn off the television and read twice as many books. In just a few sentences, Gifford has made some rather crucial commentaries on the future state of television.

KRESIN ON KRESKIN

Those of you who have followed my career know that I have never claimed any special supernatural powers. I have always insisted that what I do is accomplished by natural and scientific means. I am not a fortuneteller -- I am a thought reader. My gift has enabled me to tune in on the thoughts of those who would cooperate and give me their attention. It has therefore been a dramatic challenge in my career when I am asked to predict a specific target or the results of a contest, whether it be in the sports or political arenas. Certainly magicians and mind reading acts have faked doing such things, but that has not been my modus operandi.

For example, In 1977, the CNN Television News people came to me with the premise of attempting to predict the results of the Academy Awards. I had done the same thing a number of years before, but was reluctant to repeat the challenge since it had taken me dozens of hours to enumerate what I felt would be the winners. When CNN asked, however, I took it upon myself once more to accept the challenge. The day before the awards ceremony, I appeared on CNN and handed them a sealed envelope containing my predictions. I was to appear on CNN Morning News the day after the Oscars to open the envelope and see how accurate I was. To ensure against some second rate magician claiming that it was some trick with switched envelopes or tampering, I showed an additional copy of my predictions to a producer on camera. After she read my predictions to herself, I burned the extra copy and left her with the sealed envelope. I was afraid if my predictions were broadcast before the Awards, some people might bet big money on the outcome based on my predictions. If I was wrong, I didn't want to be responsible for their loss. I was assured by the producer that she would not share my predictions with anyone. For added backup, I sent via special delivery, another copy of the predictions to a reporter with the admonition not to open the package until after the awards.

As it turned out, I successfully predicted the top nine categories. The question is always, "How did he do it?" I did not do it with sleight of hand, hypnosis or gimmicks. I had poured over hundreds of columnist's and critic's commentaries on the various movies, sampled them, and weighed them. I noticed which -columnists seemed to be prone to successfully picking certain categories of movies. All of them, however, had their own theories. In the end I had to use my own gut feeling and intuition. On national TV, it was an awful risk.

Another example of my ability to predict came a year later. In the beginning of 1998, as I had done for five years, I guested on CNN. I typically appeared on New Year's Eve or New Year's Day, but because of my tour schedule I appeared on January 2nd . The reason for my yearly appearance is to comment on the passing scene and the changes I think will unfold in various areas of society. Since I travel most of the year, I have the opportunity of meeting people of all walks of life and hearing about their worries and enthusiasms. On this particular day I was at the CNN set in New York and they were asking me about my blackjack successes and the topic of lotteries came up. I pointed out that the lottery was simply a crapshoot and a waste of money. However, I mentioned the number 22. 1 wasn't sure why I was thinking about 22. The host asked me what the number meant, and I told him that 22 or 222 and one other number was in my head. I wasn't sure. I was thinking about 222 and a fourth number. I got an ice cold chill after saying that and after the show was over I went up to the producer and apologized for bringing up the numbers. He looked at me and laughed. He said, "My God, we're getting calls from everywhere -all over the world -- it's caused a lot of interest." People wanted to know what the numbers meant and how they could be applied. I forgot about it and went home. Two days later I got a calls on my answering machine and newspaper clippings from New York sent to me. The clippings were for the pick four that was drawn hours after my appearance. The winning numbers were 2-2-3-2. 1 cannot even begin to estimate how many people I met in the ensuing weeks and months who told me that they had heard the remark and gone out and bet the lottery. Knowing that one number was missing, they made a few bets. Some had won over a thousand dollars! Again, this was done without trickery or gimmicks. The only answer a professional skeptic would come up with   is   that   my   prediction   was   just   chance.   Bull!

After that appearance, I made up my mind to never again play with numbers on radio or television. People ran out and bet based on my predictions and I didn't want to be responsible if they lost their money. However, on October 5, 1998, 1 was being interviewed by Dewire and Michaels, who have an extraordinarily popular talk show in Rock Island on 0106 FM. The station is a combination of talk and classic rock. I have appeared with them on a number of occasions, but this time I was giving the interview over the phone, as I was across the country preparing for an appearance the next day. They had heard the story of the Pick 4 from New York and were urging me to come up with numbers. I was reacting back to them in a joking manner pointing out that I had actually only predicted three of the four numbers. They repeatedly asked me the three numbers, and I kept reminding them that the numbers were 222. They kept asking for another number and I tried to double talk myself out of the situation until I innocently said the number 7. They repeated and clarified that I had said 2227 and frankly, I didn't want to talk about it anymore so we went on to other things. The next day I did my show and the following morning I was at the front desk checking out when a call came in to the hotel. The call was from Dewire and Michaels and they told the desk clerk that they had to interview me immediately, they were going live in minutes. I got on the phone and as they began to explain the situation. I opened the newspaper to verify the story, and sure enough, the day after my prediction, the Pick 4 was 2-2-2-7.

I doubt if you will ever hear me joke about a series of numbers on any radio or talk show again. I cannot explain how the two times I have attempted to predict lottery numbers I was exactly accurate. I simply cannot explain what happened. However, to say that it was chance is an abuse of reason. I cannot expect anyone to swallow such an inane piece of irrationality, and yet I do not understand what happened.

What follows are my predictions for the millennium. Take the opportunity to reflect upon them and use them as a creative starting point for making your own predictions.

1. When this book is published, the governments of the Western World will have still failed to notify their people that we are in another war. The enemy is using the most invisible and insidious of tactics -- that of terrorism. The gravest danger the world has faced in the last 100 years will be showing its ugly face before long. With the ominous possibilities of biological warfare, safety zones will inevitably be set up in schools and government buildings.

2. One of the three historic networks of the United States will go out of business.

3. Clinical psychologists and their therapeutic techniques will diminish in popularity and success.

4. Religions will expand to an extraordinary degree and proliferate throughout the land.

5. A Kennedy will return a feeling of Camelot to the White House within 20 years -- don't be surprised if the Kennedy is a female.

6. Criminals who have had a past history of violent acts will wear, upon release from prison, brain-tracking devices to alert law enforcement officials of any evil thoughts that could trigger new crimes.

7. Children will also wear tracking devices that emit a sound or could be a communications device linked to police stations as protection against depraved criminals.

8. Drugs will be legalized. Because it will take the profit out of drug traffic, this will be a tremendous blow to the criminal drug cartels and other organized crime organizations, as well as certain political interests.

9. HO, HO, HO will be replaced with NO, NO, NO when overprotective politicians pass legislation that will make it a

crime for anxious kiddies to sit on Santa's lap during Christmas season.

10.   Homosexuality will become a universally accepted lifestyle. This will present some rather interesting problems for them. Throughout history there has always been scapegoats of the political and mob movements. First, lepers were the scourge of society. As centuries passed, gypsies became the brunt of scathing denunciation. More time passed and the Jewish people became the targets, especially at the hands of Hitler's Nazi Germany. In the Western World, black people became the victims of judgment. One wonders what people will be the scapegoats of the new millennium. Targets seem necessary in society as a method of people avoiding the fact that they have failed in some way. These failures develop a need to pass judgment on the lives of others. It is impossible to guess which group will be the future's target. It might be refreshing if it were attorneys! It could be some ethnic group, or even aliens. Only time will tell. One thing is for certain -- there will be another scapegoat pulled out of the hat in the next millennium.

11.   A controversy will finally be resolved when it will be clearly proved that plants have "feelings" and some kind of thought. The dilemma will be, "what will the vegetarians do?"

12.   Younger students will band together in common thought, demanding that some of the extraordinary theories of scientists should require extraordinary proof. An example is the "Big Bang" theory of creation. If all that we have started with an explosion, who started the explosion? If matter always existed to explode, who created it?

13.   Since I have questioned the existence of "hypnosis" for over 30 years and do not believe there is any evidence of a hypnotic state or trance, it will not surprise me if in the coming millennium "hypnosis" will be discarded and eventually forgotten.

14.   The skeptical movements which seem to be coming out of the woodwork all around us in modern society will diminish and become laughable. Can you imagine anything more silly than to be described as a "professional skeptic?" It's almost a contradiction. How can you honestly make a living with a mind set. Is there a professional optimist? Or a professional pessimist? The entire area will be more and more suited for comedy and satire rather than taken seriously.

15.   Telepathy will again be universally accepted, as it was in the past. This will be despite the fact that it will always be difficult to prove "scientifically." Indeed, science may never be able to prove scientifically the existence of love.

Especially,

Kreskin

A
Agassi, Andre
Ailes, Roger
Aldren, Buzz
Allen, Steve
B
Baker, Paul
Berkowitz, David
Blazer, Paul
Brandman, Barry
Brenner, David
Brothers, Dr. Joyce
Browne, Chris
Bush, Casey
C
Caruba, Alan
Clark, Dick
Cote & Hall
Collins, Robert
Crandall, Jr., Clifford C.
D
DeCordova, Freddie
Diller, Phyllis
E
Ebert, Roger
Eckstein, Warren
F
Farber, Barry
Ferry, Ray
Fish, Marvin
Fish, Seymour, DDS
Ford, Whitey
Freidman, Arthur
G
Gambling, John
Garvey, Steve
Gifford, Kathie Lee
Godfrey, Arthur
Greenspan, Alan
H
Hackett, Buddy
Haffner, Debra W.
Haig, Jr., Alexander M.
Hanks, Tom
Helton, Larry
Henderson, Skitch
J
Jenner, Bruce
Johnson, Magic
Jones, Chuck
Jones, Dr. Lucy
K
Kasem, Casey
Kurtz, Dr. Paul

L
LaRosa, Julius
LaSorda, Tommy
Linkletter, Art
Livolsi, Father Joseph
Luntz, Benjamin
M
MacRobert, Alan M.
McMahon, Ed
Meglin, Nick
Meyer, David
Michaels, Marilyn
Miller, Barry A.
P
Peale, Ruth Stafford
Philbin, Regis
Piazza, Mike
Pohl, Frederik
Porter, Raymond
Puck, Wolfgang
R
Redfeather, Shifu Robert
Reynolds, Burt
Rhoades, Ed
Robertson, Pat
Romero, John
Roseanne
S
Schwarz,M.D., Berthold E.
Seinfeld, Jerry
Sharan, Farida
Satcher, M.D.,Ph.D., David
Shatner, William
Shaw, Artie
Schulz, Charles M.
Silverstone, Alicia
Slavick, Melvin
Smith, Sally E.
Springer, Jerry
Starr, Kenneth
Stern, Howard
Stossel, John
Suchin, Milt
Sunnen, M.D., Gerard V.
T
Teller, Dr. Edward
Thomas, Clarence
Thomas, Phil
U
Utian, M.D., Ph.D., Wulf H.
V
Vorisek, John F.
W
Waldron, Dan
Williams, Dian
Williams, Terrie